HEALTHY MEAL PREP COOKBOOK

Nourish, Thrive & Save Time – 1000 Days of Recipes for Balanced, Vibrant Living

Ethan Perry

Table of Contents

Introduction

1. Introduction to the Healthy Meal Prep Cookbook

Hello and welcome, fellow food enthusiasts! I'm Ethan Perry, and this is the "Healthy Meal Prep Cookbook" – your personal guide to a world where health meets taste, and convenience meets nutrition.

As someone who's journeyed through the bustling streets of the UK, the diverse landscapes of the US, and the culinary-rich regions of Italy, I've learned one universal truth: the way we eat profoundly impacts our lives. This book is more than just a collection of recipes; it's a reflection of a lifestyle, a testament to the belief that good food is the cornerstone of vibrant living.

This cookbook is a culmination of my experiences and learnings, a response to the fast-paced world we live in. It's for you – the busy parent, the working professional, the health-conscious individual, and everyone in between. Inside, you'll find a range of recipes to suit various dietary needs, including vegetarian (VGT), vegan (VGN), meat and fish dishes. Each recipe is crafted to make your meal prep journey simpler, healthier, and absolutely delicious.

But it's not just about the recipes. It's about understanding the why and how – why meal prepping can transform your life and how you can do it effectively. From tips on saving time and money to reducing waste and understanding the importance of kitchen hygiene, this book is a comprehensive guide designed to navigate you through the art of meal preparation. You'll also find insights into substituting ingredients for healthier alternatives, like using shirataki noodles instead of regular pasta or opting for natural sweeteners over refined sugar. It's all about making choices that fit your lifestyle and preferences while keeping health at the forefront. So, as you turn these pages and embark on this culinary journey, remember that each recipe, tip, and piece of advice is geared towards enhancing your life, one meal at a time. Here's to cooking that's as enjoyable as it is nourishing, as convenient as it is satisfying. Welcome to the "Healthy Meal Prep Cookbook" – where your healthiest self begins in the kitchen.
Let's get prepping!
Ethan Perry

2. Disclaimer

This book, "Healthy Meal Prep Cookbook" by Ethan Perry, is intended to provide helpful and informative material on the subjects of meal preparation, cooking, and nutrition. It is sold with the understanding that the author and publisher are not engaged in rendering medical, health, psychological, or any other kind of personal professional services through this book. The recipes and tips within are provided as suggestions only and should not replace the advice of a healthcare professional. Please note that the caloric and nutritional content specified in the recipes of this book are approximations only. While we strive to provide accurate and helpful nutritional information, these estimates should not be considered exact or definitive. Variations in ingredient choices, portion sizes, preparation techniques, and the inherent diversity in natural food products mean actual nutritional values may vary.

While every effort has been made to ensure the accuracy and effectiveness of the information and recipes in this cookbook, the author and publisher expressly disclaim responsibility for any adverse effects that may result from the use or application of the recipes and information contained herein.

The author and publisher are not responsible for any injuries, damages, or negative consequences from any treatment, action, application, preparation, or interpretation by any person following the information in this book. The use of this information should be based on your own due diligence and judgment in consultation with professional medical advice.

It is the reader's responsibility to ensure that their food preparation area is safe, that they are aware of any potential food allergens, and that they practice safe food handling. The author and publisher are not liable for any incidents of foodborne illness, allergic reactions, or any other incidents arising from the use of the recipes in this book.

3. Kitchen Hygiene: Keeping It Clean and Safe

A clean kitchen is the foundation of healthy cooking. By maintaining good hygiene practices, you can prevent contamination and ensure that your meals are not only delicious but also safe to eat. Here's what you need to know:

Cutting Boards

Choose Wisely: Use non-porous cutting boards, such as those made from plastic or tempered glass, for raw meat, poultry, and seafood to prevent bacteria from soaking in.

Separation is Key: Have separate cutting boards for fresh produce and raw meats to avoid cross-contamination.

Regular Cleaning: Wash cutting boards with hot soapy water after each use. For a deeper clean, use a mixture of bleach and water (1 tablespoon of bleach per gallon of water) to sanitize them.

Replace When Necessary: Over time, cutting boards can develop deep grooves where bacteria can hide. Replace any cutting boards that have become excessively worn or have deep cuts.Wear and Tear on Pans

Non-Stick Cookware: If you use non-stick pans, avoid using metal utensils that can scratch and damage the surface. Once the coating starts peeling, it's time to replace the pan to prevent flakes from getting into your food.

Regular Inspection: Check all cookware for signs of wear, such as rust, chipping, or cracking. Damaged cookware can harbor bacteria and may also affect the quality and safety of your food.

Proper Cleaning: Clean your pans after each use with hot soapy water. For stubborn residue, soak the pan and use a non-abrasive sponge to prevent damage to the surface.

Cleaning of Surfaces

Disinfect Regularly: Wipe down countertops, stove, and kitchen appliances with a disinfectant cleaner before and after cooking. Pay special attention to areas that have come into contact with raw meat, poultry, or seafood.

Use Separate Cloths: Use separate cloths or sponges for dishes and surfaces to avoid cross-contamination. Regularly replace or sanitize these items, as they can be breeding grounds for bacteria.

Immediate Spills Response: Clean up spills immediately to prevent bacteria from spreading and to avoid attracting pests.

General Tips

Wash Your Hands: Always wash your hands with soap and water for at least 20 seconds before handling food, after touching raw meat, and after using the bathroom.

Food Storage: Keep your refrigerator below 4°C (40°F) and your freezer at -18°C (0°F) to slow bacterial growth. Store raw meat on the bottom shelf to prevent juices from dripping onto other foods.

Regular Maintenance: Regularly clean and service your kitchen appliances according to the manufacturer's instructions to ensure they are working correctly and efficiently.

Pest Control: Keep your kitchen free from pests, which can spread bacteria. Store food in airtight containers and dispose of garbage regularly.

By following these guidelines, you can create a kitchen environment that's not just conducive to cooking delicious meals, but also one that prioritizes the health and safety of everyone who enjoys them. A clean kitchen is the secret ingredient to every successful meal prep!

4. The Benefits of Food Preparation

Saving Time and Reducing Stress

Efficient Use of Time: One of the most immediate benefits of meal prep is the time it saves. By dedicating a few hours to preparing meals for the week, you save daily time otherwise spent cooking. This efficiency frees up your schedule, allowing you to focus on other important activities or simply relax.

Reduced Decision Fatigue: Knowing what you're going to eat in advance eliminates the daily stress of deciding and preparing meals. This planned approach can significantly reduce mental load and decision fatigue.

Healthier Eating Habits

Portion Control: Preparing your meals in advance helps with portion control, a key factor in maintaining a healthy weight and diet. By deciding portions when you're not hungry, you're more likely to serve the amount your body needs.

Balanced Nutrition: Meal prep allows you to plan a balanced diet that includes a variety of nutrients. You can ensure that every meal has the right balance of proteins, fats, and carbohydrates, as well as vitamins and minerals.

Avoid Unhealthy Choices: When you're hungry and short on time, you're more likely to grab fast food or processed snacks. Having a prepared meal ready to go is the best defense against reaching for unhealthy options.

Economical Benefits

Budget-Friendly: Meal prep is cost-effective. Buying ingredients in bulk often costs less than purchasing small portions. You can also minimize waste by using all the ingredients you've bought for your planned meals.

Less Impulse Buying: When you shop with a meal plan in mind, you're less likely to make impulse purchases. This not only saves money but also ensures that you're buying foods that contribute to your health goals.

Enhancing Your Culinary Skills

Skill Improvement: Regular meal prep is a great way to improve your cooking skills. As you become more comfortable in the kitchen, you'll learn to make meals more efficiently and try new, adventurous recipes.

Creative Exploration: Planning your meals doesn't mean eating the same thing every day. It encourages you to explore new recipes and ingredients, keeping your diet interesting and diverse.

Social and Family Benefits

Family Involvement: Meal prep can be a family activity, offering a great way to spend time together and teach children about healthy eating and cooking.

Social Eating: Having meals ready means you can easily entertain guests or contribute to potlucks and gatherings without the added stress of last-minute cooking.

Environmental Impact

Reduced Waste: By planning and preparing exact portions, you're less likely to have food spoilage. This not only saves money but also reduces food waste, benefiting the environment.

Mindful Consumption: Meal prepping encourages mindfulness about food sources, seasonality, and sustainability, promoting a more environmentally friendly approach to eating.

Sustaining Long-Term Health Goals

Consistent Healthy Choices: Meal prep makes it easier to stick to healthy eating goals over time. By removing daily obstacles and planning, individuals are more likely to maintain a nutritious diet, contributing to long-term health and wellness.

Adaptable to Dietary Needs: Whether you're managing a specific health condition, following a dietary restriction, or working toward a fitness goal, meal prep allows you to tailor your diet to meet those needs consistently.

Reducing Environmental Footprint

Mindful Packaging: By using reusable containers and minimizing single-use plastics, meal preppers can significantly reduce their environmental impact. Choosing sustainable packaging options contributes to a healthier planet.

Lowering Carbon Footprint: Planning meals can lead to reduced trips to the grocery store, which means fewer car journeys and a lower carbon footprint. Additionally, by being mindful of food sources and choosing local and seasonal ingredients, you can further reduce the environmental impact of your meals.

Enhancing Mental Well-being

Reduced Anxiety: Knowing your meals are prepared and ready to go can reduce anxiety and stress related to mealtime, especially for those with busy schedules or health concerns that require strict dietary adherence.

Increased Satisfaction: There's a deep sense of satisfaction in eating a home-cooked meal that you've prepared. This act of self-care can boost mood and increase feelings of well-being.

5. Incorporating Meal Prep into Your Lifestyle

Starting Small

Baby Steps: If you're new to meal prepping, start small. Begin by preparing just one type of meal, like breakfast or lunch, and gradually add more as you become comfortable.

Simple Recipes: Choose recipes that are simple and familiar. As your confidence grows, you can start experimenting with more complex dishes.

Organizing Your Kitchen

Essential Tools: Having the right tools can make meal prep more efficient. Invest in quality knives, cutting boards, storage containers, and appliances like slow cookers, air fryer or blenders.

Kitchen Layout: Organize your kitchen so that frequently used items are easily accessible. A well-organized space makes the cooking process smoother and more enjoyable.

Making It Enjoyable

Enjoy the Process: Find ways to make meal prep enjoyable. Listen to music, podcasts, or audiobooks while you cook, or turn it into a family activity.

Visual Appeal: Make your meals visually appealing. The more attractive your food is, the more likely you are to enjoy it. Experiment with colors, textures, and garnishes.

Adjusting As Needed

Flexibility: Life is unpredictable. If your schedule changes or you don't feel like eating what you've prepared, it's okay to adjust. Meal prep should fit into your life, not the other way around.

Feedback and Iteration: Pay attention to what works and what doesn't. Maybe certain dishes don't reheat well, or you find you prefer more variety. Use this feedback to continually refine your meal prep process.

Maximizing the Potential of Recipes: A Guide to Personalized Cooking: Unlock the full potential of every recipe by embracing the freedom to adapt them to your preferences. For instance, if you encounter a recipe featuring cheese but adhere to a vegan lifestyle, don't hesitate to substitute it with a plant-based alternative. Remember, cooking is an art form, a creative expression that thrives on experimentation and personal touches. To elevate your culinary creations, prioritize the use of high-quality ingredients. Whenever possible, source your produce directly from local farmers or small-scale producers. This not only supports sustainable practices but also ensures that your ingredients are free from harmful preservatives, benefiting both the food's flavor and your health. Embrace this approach, and transform every meal into a nourishing masterpiece."

6. Choosing the Best Containers for Your Meal Prep

As you embark on your meal prep journey, one crucial aspect to consider is the type of containers you use to store your food. The right containers not only keep your meals fresh but also ensure they're safe to eat after storage in the fridge or freezer. Here's what you need to know about selecting the best options for your needs.

BPA-Free Plastic Containers: If you prefer something lighter, BPA-free plastic containers are your go-to. Ensure they are labeled as BPA-free and are also microwave-safe and dishwasher-safe for convenience.

Glass Containers: Glass is a fantastic option for meal prep. It doesn't absorb flavors or smells, is generally safe to clean in the dishwasher, and can go in the microwave without concern. Look for glass containers with airtight lids to keep your food fresh.

Stainless Steel Containers: Durable and long-lasting, stainless steel containers are an excellent choice for those avoiding plastic. They're typically not microwave-safe but are great for storing in the fridge or freezer.

Silicone Containers: Collapsible silicone containers can be a space-saving solution. They are generally safe for use in microwaves, ovens, and freezers, making them versatile for various meal prep scenarios.

Considerations for Choosing Containers

Size and Shape: Have a variety of sizes to accommodate everything from large batches of soups and stews to individual portions. Consider the shape as well, as some might fit better in your fridge or freezer.

Leak-proof and Airtight: To keep your meals as fresh as possible and avoid spills, opt for containers with leak-proof and airtight seals.

Stackability: Space is often at a premium, especially in the freezer. Look for containers that stack neatly on top of each other to maximize space.

Microwave and Freezer Safe: Ensure your containers are suitable for the freezer to keep meals long-term and microwave-safe for easy reheating.

Labeling: Being able to label your containers with the contents and date prepared is incredibly helpful for keeping track of what's in your fridge or freezer and ensuring you use it while it's still at its best.

Caring for Your Containers

Regular Cleaning: Clean your containers after each use to prevent staining and odors. Most glass and BPA-free plastic containers can go in the dishwasher, but check the manufacturer's instructions first.

Inspect Regularly: Over time, containers can wear out, especially those used frequently in the microwave or freezer. Regularly inspect your containers for signs of wear and tear, and replace them as needed.

By investing in quality containers and taking good care of them, you can ensure that your meal prep is not just convenient and delicious but also safe and healthy. The right containers are more than just a storage solution; they're an integral part of your meal prep success.

7. Food Storage Guidelines for Refrigerator and Freezer

Food Item	Refrigerator Storage	Refrigerator Shelf Life	Freezer Storage	Freezer Shelf Life	Additional Notes
Cooked Fish	Airtight containers	3-4 days	Tightly wrapped or in freezer-safe containers	4-6 months	
Salad (without dressing)	Airtight containers	3-5 days	Not recommended	Not applicable	Salads with dressing should be consumed within 1-2 days
Cooked Meat	Shallow airtight containers or tightly wrapped	3-4 days	Heavy-duty aluminum foil, freezer wrap, or freezer bags	2-3 months	
Cooked Vegetables	Airtight containers	3-5 days	Covered airtight containers or heavy-duty freezer bags	2-3 months	
Soups and Stews	Airtight containers	3-4 days	Airtight containers or heavy-duty freezer bags	2-3 months	

Notes:
Always cool your food to room temperature before refrigerating or freezing.
Divide meals into portion-sized containers for easy reheating.
Label your containers with the date of storage.
Regularly check your refrigerator and freezer temperatures to ensure they are at the correct settings.

Do you want to refreeze something that has been defrosted from the freezer?

Here are some general guidelines:
Defrosted in the Refrigerator: If you thawed the item in the refrigerator and it hasn't been sitting out at room temperature, it's generally safe to refreeze it within a day or two of thawing, as long as it hasn't spoiled. The quality may deteriorate due to moisture loss, leading to a drier texture and less flavor.

Defrosted in Cold Water or Microwave: If the item was thawed in cold water or in the microwave, it should be cooked immediately after thawing and should only be refrozen after it has been cooked. This is because these methods can bring parts of the food into the "danger zone" (between 40°F and 140°F) where bacteria can multiply rapidly.

Raw vs. Cooked: Cooked food that has been thawed in the refrigerator can be refrozen more safely than raw food. However, the quality may still suffer.

Quality and Safety: Each time food is frozen, the quality may decrease, so it's best to only refreeze items if necessary. Also, never refreeze anything that has been left out at room temperature for more than 2 hours, or 1 hour if the temperature is above 90°F.

Seafood and Meat: Be extra cautious with seafood and meats, especially if they've been thawed using a quick method. It's usually better to cook them immediately and then freeze the cooked dish.

Taste and Texture: Be prepared for possible changes in taste and texture. Some items, especially those with high moisture content, may become mushy or lose flavor.

In all cases, ensure that the food is still of good quality and hasn't spoiled before deciding to refreeze it. When in doubt, do not refreeze.

8. Tips on How To Drop Calories

Shirataki Noodles: Use them instead of Regular Pasta
Why Use Shirataki Noodles: Shirataki noodles are a low-calorie, low-carbohydrate alternative to traditional pasta. Made from the konjac plant, they contain a type of fiber called glucomannan, which can aid in weight loss and improve digestion.

Tips:

Rinse Well: Shirataki noodles have a distinct odor when packaged; rinsing them well under cold water can remove this smell.

Dry Roast: To improve texture, dry roast the noodles in a non-stick pan until they become slightly firmer.

Pair with Flavorful Sauces: Since shirataki noodles don't have much taste, they pair well with robust sauces and seasonings.

My favorites are with bolognese sauce or with pesto. Try them that way, too, or with vegan cheese or garlic, oil and chili.

Olive Oil Instead of Butter

Why Use Olive Oil: Olive oil is a heart-healthy fat rich in antioxidants and monounsaturated fats. It can help lower bad cholesterol levels and has anti-inflammatory properties.

Tips:

Use in Cooking: Substitute butter with olive oil in sautéing and roasting. Use a 3:4 ratio, meaning for every tablespoon of butter, use three-quarters of a tablespoon of olive oil.

Baking: When baking, use a 1:1 ratio, but expect a slightly different texture and flavor. Olive oil makes baked goods moister and denser.

I often use Xylitol (is a sugar alcohol with a sweetness) similar to sugar but with about 40% fewer calories. It doesn't spike blood sugar or insulin levels, making it a healthier alternative, especially for people with diabetes.

Tips:

Similar Sweetness: Use xylitol in the same amount as you would sugar as its sweetness is quite comparable.

Dental Benefits: Xylitol can help reduce the risk of tooth decay, making it a good option for sweetening beverages.

Digestive Considerations: Introduce xylitol slowly into your diet, as overconsumption can lead to digestive discomfort.

Other Healthy Substitutes

Greek Yogurt for Sour Cream or Mayonnaise: Rich in protein and probiotics, Greek yogurt is an excellent substitute for sour cream or mayonnaise in dips, spreads, and dressings.

Almond/Coconut Milk for Cow's Milk: For those lactose intolerant or looking to reduce dairy, almond and coconut milk are great alternatives in recipes.

Cauliflower Rice for White Rice: To reduce carbs and increase vegetable intake, use cauliflower rice as a substitute for white or brown rice.

General Tips for Substituting Ingredients

Start Gradually: If you're new to using substitutes, start by replacing a portion of the ingredient rather than the whole amount to gradually adjust to the taste and texture differences.

Consider Nutritional Needs: Always choose substitutes that align with your dietary needs and preferences. What works for one person may not work for another.

Experiment and Adjust: Be prepared to experiment and make adjustments as necessary. Substitutes can sometimes change the flavor, texture, or appearance of your dish, so it might take a few tries to get it right.

Incorporating these substitutes into your meal prep can lead to healthier eating habits without sacrificing taste. As you explore these alternatives, you'll not only improve your nutritional intake but also expand your culinary repertoire.

9. Vegetables and Their Role in Your Prep

Dear Readers,

"Incorporating vegetables as a core component of your meals is not only a nutritious choice but also a strategic way to reduce calorie intake while still satisfying your hunger. Consider swapping out heavier meal components with a variety of colorful, fiber-rich vegetables. This switch can be particularly beneficial after periods of indulgent eating or when you're looking to shed some extra calories without compromising on taste or fullness

Vegetables are nutritional powerhouses packed with vitamins, minerals, fiber, and antioxidants while being low in calories. They are essential for a balanced diet and can significantly contribute to your health and well-being.To help you incorporate more vegetables into your meals, we've compiled a list of low-calorie options. These can be enjoyed alongside your main dishes, added to your meal preps, or consumed as a healthy morning or afternoon snack.

Recommended Low-Calorie Vegetables

Here's a list of nutrient-dense, low-calorie vegetables that we recommend incorporating into your daily meals:

Spinach: Rich in iron, calcium, and vitamins A and C, spinach is a versatile leafy green that can be added to salads, smoothies, omelets, and more.

Broccoli: Packed with fiber, vitamin C, and a variety of nutrients, broccoli can be steamed, roasted, or stir-fried.

Cauliflower: Low in calories but high in fiber and vitamins, cauliflower can be roasted, turned into cauliflower rice, or even used as a pizza crust.

Zucchini: Great for stir-fries, zoodles (zucchini noodles), and baking, zucchini is a low-calorie vegetable that can add volume to your meals.

Bell Peppers: High in vitamin C and antioxidants, bell peppers can be enjoyed raw, roasted, or stuffed.

Cucumber: With high water content and low calories, cucumbers are perfect for hydration and can be enjoyed in salads or as a refreshing snack.

Tomatoes: While technically a fruit, tomatoes are commonly consumed as a vegetable and offer vitamin C, potassium, and lycopene.

Kale: A nutrient powerhouse, kale can be used in salads, smoothies, or baked into chips.

Asparagus: Rich in folate and vitamins A, C, and K, asparagus can be grilled, roasted, or steamed.

Green Beans: Low in calories and high in fiber, green beans can be steamed, sautéed, or added to casseroles.

By making vegetables a constant presence in your meals, you're not only enhancing the flavor and variety of your dishes but also significantly boosting your nutritional intake. We encourage you to embrace the versatility and health benefits of vegetables and make them a cornerstone of your meal prep and daily eating habits. In the next chapters, we'll dive into the recipes themselves, starting with Vegan (VGN) dishes, followed by Vegetarian (VGT), Meat-based, and Fish selections. Each recipe is not only a guide to creating a tasty dish but also an opportunity to learn and embrace the meal prep lifestyle.

Let's turn the page and begin our culinary adventure together!

All the Recipes are Serving for 6.

Vegan Breakfast Recipes

1. VGN Peanut Butter and Banana Smoothie

Prep: 5 min | Cook: 0 min | Total: 5 min

Ingredients:

3 ripe bananas
6 tbsp peanut butter (unsweetened and unsalted)
3 cups unsweetened almond milk
1 1/2 cups ice cubes
3 tsp vanilla extract
Optional: 3 tsp maple syrup (for added sweetness)

Instructions:

In a blender, combine the bananas, peanut butter, almond milk, ice cubes, maple syrup and vanilla extract.
Blend on high speed until smooth and creamy, ensuring there are no lumps.
Taste and adjust the sweetness if necessary by adding a little more maple syrup.
Pour the smoothie into six glasses and serve immediately, or pour into airtight containers and store in the refrigerator for up to 2 days.

Nutritional Information (per serving):

Calories: Approximately 250 kcal
Protein: 8 g
Fat: 16 g
Carbohydrates: 20 g
Fiber: 4 g
Sugar: 10 g (natural sugars from banana)

2. VGN Chia Seed and Berry Pudding

Prep: 10 min | Cook: 0 min (Refrigerate overnight) | Total: 10 min + refrigeration

Ingredients:

6 cups unsweetened almond milk
1 1/2 cups chia seeds
3 tbsp maple syrup
1 1/2 tsp vanilla extract
3 cups mixed berries (strawberries, blueberries, raspberries)

Instructions:

In a large bowl, whisk together the almond milk, chia seeds, maple syrup, and vanilla extract until well combined.
Let the mixture sit for 5 minutes, then whisk again to prevent the chia seeds from clumping.
Cover the bowl and refrigerate for at least 2 hours or overnight, until the pudding achieves a thick and creamy consistency.
Before serving, stir the pudding and divide it into six serving dishes.
Top each serving with a portion of mixed berries.
Serve immediately, or cover and store in the refrigerator for up to 3 days.

Nutritional Information (per serving):

Calories: Approximately 300 kcal
Protein: 8 g
Fat: 14 g
Carbohydrates: 35 g
Fiber: 15 g
Sugar: 15 g

3. VGN Toasted Oats with Maple Syrup and Fruit

Prep: 5 min | Cook: 10 min | Total: 15 min

Ingredients:

3 cups rolled oats
6 cups almond milk (unsweetened)
3 tbsp maple syrup, plus extra for serving
1 1/2 tsp ground cinnamon
1 1/2 tsp vanilla extract
3 cups mixed fresh fruit (such as berries, sliced bananas, and apple chunks)

Instructions:

In a large saucepan, combine the rolled oats and almond milk. Bring to a simmer over medium heat.
Reduce the heat and cook the oats for 10-15 minutes, stirring occasionally, until they are soft and the liquid is mostly absorbed.
Stir in the maple syrup, cinnamon, and vanilla extract. Cook for an additional 2-3 minutes.
Remove from heat and let the oatmeal cool slightly. It will thicken upon standing.
Divide the oatmeal into six serving bowls.
Top each bowl with a portion of the mixed fresh fruit.
Drizzle additional maple syrup over each serving, according to taste.
Serve warm, or allow to cool completely and store in the refrigerator for up to 3 days.

Nutritional Information (per serving):

Calories: Approximately 300 kcal
Protein: 8 g
Fat: 7 g
Carbohydrates: 50 g
Fiber: 8 g
Sugar: 15 g

4. VGN Blueberry Muffins

Prep: 15 min | Cook: 20 min | Total: 35 min

Ingredients:

2 1/2 cups all-purpose flour
1 cup sugar
1/2 cup vegetable oil
1 cup almond milk
2 tsp baking powder
1/2 tsp salt
1 tsp vanilla extract
2 cups fresh blueberries

Instructions:

Preheat the oven to 375°F (190°C) and line a muffin tin with paper liners.
In a large bowl, mix together flour, sugar, baking powder, and salt.
In another bowl, whisk together vegetable oil, almond milk, and vanilla extract.
Gradually add the wet ingredients to the dry ingredients, stirring until just combined.
Gently fold in the blueberries.
Divide the batter evenly among the muffin cups, filling each about 3/4 full.
Bake for 20-25 minutes, or until a toothpick inserted into the center comes out clean.
Allow to cool in the tin for 5 minutes, then transfer to a wire rack to cool completely.
Store in an airtight container for up to 3 days.

Nutritional Information (per muffin):

Calories: Approximately 200 kcal
Protein: 3 g
Fat: 8 g
Carbohydrates: 30 g
Fiber: 1 g
Sugar: 15 g

5. VGN Tofu and Vegetable Scramble

Prep: 10 min | Cook: 15 min | Total: 25 min

Ingredients:

1 block (14 oz) firm tofu, drained and crumbled
2 tbsp olive oil
1 onion, diced
1 bell pepper, diced
1 cup spinach, chopped
2 tomatoes, diced
1 tsp turmeric
Salt and pepper to taste

Instructions:

Heat olive oil in a large skillet over medium heat.
Add the onion and bell pepper, sautéing until softened.
Stir in the crumbled tofu and turmeric. Cook for 5 minutes, stirring occasionally.
Add the spinach and tomatoes, cooking until the spinach is wilted.
Season with salt and pepper to taste.
Divide the scramble among six plates.
Serve hot, or let cool and store in the refrigerator for up to 3 days.

Nutritional Information (per serving):

Calories: Approximately 150 kcal
Protein: 10 g
Fat: 10 g
Carbohydrates: 8 g
Fiber: 2 g
Sugar: 3 g

6. VGN Almond Milk and Fruit Porridge

Prep: 5 min | Cook: 15 min | Total: 20 min

Ingredients:

3 cups rolled oats
6 cups unsweetened almond milk
3 tbsp maple syrup
1 tsp cinnamon
3 cups mixed fresh fruit (berries, sliced banana, apple)

Instructions:

In a large saucepan, combine the oats and almond milk. Bring to a simmer over medium heat.
Cook, stirring frequently, for 10-15 minutes or until the oats are soft and the mixture has thickened.
Stir in the maple syrup and cinnamon.
Remove from heat and let sit for a few minutes to thicken further.
Serve the porridge in bowls, topped with fresh fruit.
Store any leftovers in the refrigerator for up to 3 days.

Nutritional Information (per serving):

Calories: Approximately 250 kcal
Protein: 6 g
Fat: 7 g
Carbohydrates: 40 g
Fiber: 6 g
Sugar: 12 g

7. VGN Breakfast Burrito with Beans

Prep: 15 min | Cook: 10 min | Total: 25 min

Ingredients:

6 large whole wheat tortillas
2 cans (15 oz each) black beans, drained and rinsed
1 cup corn kernels (fresh or frozen)
1 red bell pepper, diced
1 onion, diced
2 avocados, sliced
1/2 cup salsa
2 tsp ground cumin
Salt and pepper to taste
1 tbsp olive oil

Instructions:

In a skillet, heat olive oil over medium heat. Add onion and bell pepper, sauté until softened.
Stir in black beans, corn, cumin, salt, and pepper. Cook for 5-7 minutes until heated through.
Warm the tortillas in a separate pan or microwave.
To assemble, divide the bean mixture among the tortillas. Top each with avocado slices and a spoonful of salsa.
Roll up the tortillas, folding in the sides to enclose the filling.
Serve immediately, or wrap each burrito in foil and refrigerate for up to 3 days.

Nutritional Information (per burrito):

Calories: Approximately 350 kcal
Protein: 12 g
Fat: 12 g
Carbohydrates: 50 g
Fiber: 10 g
Sugar: 5 g

8. VGN Sweet Potato and Black Bean Hash

Prep: 10 min | Cook: 20 min | Total: 30 min

Ingredients:

3 large sweet potatoes, peeled and diced
2 cans (15 oz each) black beans, drained and rinsed
1 large onion, diced
1 red bell pepper, diced
2 tsp smoked paprika
1 tsp cumin
Salt and pepper to taste
3 tbsp olive oil
Fresh cilantro for garnish

Instructions:

Heat 2 tablespoons of olive oil in a large skillet over medium heat. Add sweet potatoes and cook until tender and slightly caramelized, about 15 minutes.
In another skillet, heat the remaining olive oil. Add onion and bell pepper, sauté until soft.
Stir in black beans, smoked paprika, cumin, salt, and pepper. Cook for another 5 minutes.
Combine the sweet potatoes with the bean mixture. Adjust seasoning as needed.
Garnish with fresh cilantro.
Serve hot or allow to cool and store in containers. Reheat in the microwave when ready to eat.

Nutritional Information (per serving):

Calories: Approximately 300 kcal
Protein: 10 g
Fat: 8 g
Carbohydrates: 50 g
Fiber: 12 g
Sugar: 8 g

9. VGN Overnight Oats with Coconut Milk

Prep: 5 min | Cook: 0 min (Refrigerate overnight) | Total: 5 min + refrigeration

Ingredients:

3 cups rolled oats
6 cups coconut milk (unsweetened)
3 tbsp chia seeds
3 tbsp maple syrup
1 1/2 tsp vanilla extract
Toppings: Sliced bananas, berries, nuts

Instructions:

In a large bowl, mix together oats, coconut milk, chia seeds, maple syrup, and vanilla extract.
Cover and refrigerate overnight.
In the morning, stir the oats. If the mixture is too thick, add a little more coconut milk to reach your desired consistency.
Serve in bowls, topped with your choice of bananas, berries, and nuts.
Store any leftovers in the refrigerator for up to 3 days.

Nutritional Information (per serving):

Calories: Approximately 350 kcal
Protein: 10 g
Fat: 14 g
Carbohydrates: 50 g
Fiber: 10 g
Sugar: 12

10. VGN Banana Bread

Prep: 5 min | Cook: 0 min (Refrigerate overnight) | Total: 5 min + refrigeration

Ingredients:

2 1/2 cups whole wheat flour
1 cup mashed ripe bananas (about 3 medium bananas)
1/2 cup unsweetened applesauce
1/2 cup maple syrup
1/2 cup almond milk
1 tsp baking soda
1 tsp vanilla extract
1/2 tsp cinnamon
1/4 tsp salt
Optional: 1/2 cup walnuts or pecans, chopped

Instructions:

Preheat the oven to 350°F (175°C). Grease a 9x5 inch loaf pan.
In a large bowl, combine the flour, baking soda, cinnamon, and salt.
In another bowl, mix together the mashed bananas, applesauce, maple syrup, almond milk, and vanilla extract.
Add the wet ingredients to the dry ingredients and stir until just combined. Fold in nuts if using.
Pour the batter into the prepared loaf pan.
Bake for 50-60 minutes, or until a toothpick inserted into the center comes out clean.
Cool in the pan for 10 minutes, then transfer to a wire rack to cool completely.
Slice and serve, or store in an airtight container for up to 5 days.

Nutritional Information (per slice, 12 slices total):

Calories: Approximately 180 kcal
Protein: 3 g
Fat: 3 g (without nuts)
Carbohydrates: 35 g
Fiber: 4 g, Sugar: 12 g

11. VGN Quinoa and Berry Breakfast Bowl

Prep: 5 min | Cook: 20 min | Total: 25 min

Ingredients:

2 cups quinoa, cooked
2 cups mixed berries (strawberries, blueberries, raspberries)
1/4 cup maple syrup
1/2 cup almond milk
1/4 cup almonds, sliced
1 tsp cinnamon
Fresh mint for garnish

Instructions:

Divide cooked quinoa among 6 bowls.
Top each bowl with a mix of berries.
Drizzle with maple syrup and almond milk.
Sprinkle with sliced almonds and cinnamon.
Garnish with fresh mint leaves.

Nutritional Information (per serving):

Calories: Approximately 300 kcal
Protein: 8 g
Fat: 7 g
Carbohydrates: 50 g
Fiber: 6 g
Sugar: 15 g

12. VGN Apple Cinnamon Baked Oatmeal

Prep: 15 min | Cook: 40 min | Total: 55 min

Ingredients:

3 cups rolled oats
2 apples, diced
1/4 cup maple syrup
2 cups almond milk
2 tsp cinnamon
1/2 cup walnuts, chopped
1 tsp baking powder
Pinch of salt

Instructions:

Preheat the oven to 350°F (175°C). Grease a baking dish.
In a bowl, mix together oats, diced apples, cinnamon, baking powder, and salt.
Stir in almond milk and maple syrup.
Pour the mixture into the baking dish and sprinkle with chopped walnuts.
Bake for 25-30 minutes, or until set and golden.
Serve warm.

Nutritional Information (per serving):

Calories: Approximately 300 kcal
Protein: 8 g
Fat: 10 g
Carbohydrates: 45 g
Fiber: 6 g
Sugar: 15 g

13. VGN Mango and Kiwi Fruit Salad

Prep: 15 min | Cook: 0 min | Total: 15 min

Ingredients:

3 ripe mangoes, peeled and diced
6 kiwis, peeled and sliced
1/4 cup fresh lime juice
2 tbsp agave syrup
1/4 cup fresh mint, chopped
1/4 cup coconut flakes

Instructions:

In a large bowl, combine diced mangoes and sliced kiwis.
In a small bowl, whisk together lime juice and agave syrup.
Pour the dressing over the fruit and gently toss.
Sprinkle with chopped mint and coconut flakes.
Serve immediately or chill in the refrigerator before serving.

Nutritional Information (per serving):

Calories: Approximately 150 kcal
Protein: 2 g
Fat: 1 g
Carbohydrates: 35 g
Fiber: 5 g
Sugar: 30 g

14. VGN Savory Avocado and Tomato Toast

Prep: 5 min | Cook: 5 min | Total: 10 min

Ingredients:

12 slices whole-grain bread
3 ripe avocados, mashed
3 tomatoes, sliced
1/4 cup olive oil
1 lemon, juiced
Salt and pepper to taste
Red pepper flakes (optional)
Fresh cilantro for garnish

Instructions:

Toast the bread slices until golden and crispy.
In a small bowl, mix mashed avocados with lemon juice, salt, and pepper.
Spread avocado mixture on each toast slice.
Top with tomato slices. Drizzle with olive oil.
Sprinkle with red pepper flakes (if using) and garnish with cilantro.
Serve immediately.

Nutritional Information (per serving, 2 toasts):

Calories: Approximately 300 kcal
Protein: 6 g
Fat: 15 g
Carbohydrates: 35 g
Fiber: 8 g
Sugar: 5 g

15. VGN Spinach and Mushroom Breakfast Tacos

Prep: 15 min | Cook: 10 min | Total: 25 min

Ingredients:

12 corn tortillas
3 cups baby spinach
2 cups mushrooms, sliced
1 onion, diced
2 cloves garlic, minced
1 tsp cumin
Salt and pepper to taste
2 tbsp olive oil
Fresh salsa for topping
Fresh cilantro for garnish

Instructions:

In a skillet, heat olive oil over medium heat. Sauté onion and garlic until translucent.
Add mushrooms and cook until they release their moisture and start to brown.
Stir in baby spinach and cumin. Cook until spinach is wilted. Season with salt and pepper.
Warm tortillas in the oven or on a skillet.
Divide the spinach and mushroom mixture among the tortillas.
Top with fresh salsa and garnish with cilantro.
Serve immediately.

Nutritional Information (per serving, 2 tacos):

Calories: Approximately 200 kcal
Protein: 5 g
Fat: 7 g
Carbohydrates: 30 g
Fiber: 5 g
Sugar: 3 g

16. VGN Carrot and Raisin Breakfast Cookies

Prep: 20 min | Cook: 15 min | Total: 35 min

Ingredients:

2 cups rolled oats
1 cup whole wheat flour
1/2 cup raisins
1/2 cup carrots, grated
1/4 cup maple syrup
1/4 cup almond milk
1/4 cup coconut oil, melted
1 tsp cinnamon
1/2 tsp nutmeg
1/2 tsp baking soda
Pinch of salt

Instructions:

Preheat the oven to 350°F (175°C). Line a baking sheet with parchment paper.
In a large bowl, combine rolled oats, flour, raisins, grated carrots, cinnamon, nutmeg, baking soda, and salt.
Stir in maple syrup, almond milk, and melted coconut oil until well mixed.
Drop spoonfuls of the dough onto the prepared baking sheet.
Flatten slightly and bake for 15-20 minutes, or until golden brown.
Cool on a wire rack before serving.

Nutritional Information (per serving, 1 cookie):

Calories: Approximately 150 kcal
Protein: 3 g
Fat: 5 g
Carbohydrates: 25 g
Fiber: 3 g
Sugar: 10 g

Vegetarian Breakfast Recipes

17. VGT Mixed Berry Yogurt Parfait

Prep: 10 min | Cook: 0 min | Total: 10 min

Ingredients:

3 cups plain Greek yogurt
1 1/2 cups granola
3 cups mixed berries (such as strawberries, blueberries, raspberries)
6 tbsp honey or maple syrup
Optional: mint leaves for garnish

Instructions:

In six serving glasses or bowls, layer 1/4 cup of Greek yogurt at the bottom.
Add a layer of 2 tbsp granola on top of the yogurt.
Add a layer of 1/4 cup mixed berries.
Repeat the layers until all ingredients are used, finishing with a layer of berries.
Drizzle each parfait with 1 tbsp of honey or maple syrup.
Garnish with mint leaves if desired.
Serve immediately or refrigerate until ready to serve. Can be stored in the refrigerator for up to 2 days.

Nutritional Information (per serving):

Calories: Approximately 300 kcal
Protein: 15 g
Fat: 8 g
Carbohydrates: 45 g
Fiber: 4 g
Sugar: 30 g

18. VGT Spinach and Feta Omelette

Prep: 5 min | Cook: 10 min | Total: 15 min

Ingredients:

12 large eggs
2 cups fresh spinach, chopped
1 cup feta cheese, crumbled
1 medium onion, finely chopped
2 tbsp olive oil
Salt and pepper to taste

Instructions:

In a large bowl, whisk the eggs. Season with salt and pepper.
Heat 1 tbsp olive oil in a large skillet over medium heat. Sauté the onion until translucent. Add the chopped spinach to the skillet and cook until it wilts.
Pour half of the egg mixture over the spinach and onions. Cook until the edges start to set.
Sprinkle half of the feta cheese over the omelette. Fold it in half and cook until the cheese begins to melt.
Repeat the process with the remaining ingredients to make a second omelette.
Serve each omelette cut into three portions.
Store any leftovers in the refrigerator for up to 2 days.

Nutritional Information (per serving, 1/6 of the recipe):

Calories: Approximately 250 kcal, protein: 18 g,
Fat: 18 g, Carbohydrates: 4 g
Fiber: 1 g,Sugar: 2 g

19. VGT Avocado and Cheese Toast

Prep: 5 min | Cook: 5 min | Total: 10 min

Ingredients:

6 slices of whole grain bread
3 ripe avocados
1 1/2 cups shredded cheddar cheese
Salt and pepper to taste
Crushed red pepper flakes (optional)
1 lemon, juiced

Instructions:

Toast the bread slices until they are golden brown and crispy.
In a bowl, mash the avocados with a fork. Stir in lemon juice, salt, and pepper.
Spread the mashed avocado evenly on each toasted bread slice.
Top each slice with 1/4 cup of shredded cheddar cheese.
Place the toasts under a broiler for 1-2 minutes or until the cheese is melted and bubbly.
Optionally, sprinkle with crushed red pepper flakes for added spice.
Serve immediately.
If storing, keep the mashed avocado mixture in an airtight container in the refrigerator, and assemble the toasts when ready to eat. Avocado mixture can be stored for up to 2 days.

Nutritional Information (per serving):

Calories: Approximately 300 kcal
Protein: 10 g
Fat: 20 g
Carbohydrates: 25 g
Fiber: 7 g
Sugar: 3 g

20. VGT Greek Yogurt with Honey and Nuts

Prep: 5 min | Cook: 0 min | Total: 5 min

Ingredients:

3 cups Greek yogurt (plain or vanilla flavored)
6 tbsp honey
1 1/2 cups mixed nuts (such as almonds, walnuts, and pecans), chopped
Optional: fresh fruit or berries for topping

Instructions:

Divide the Greek yogurt equally into six serving bowls.
Drizzle each bowl with 1 tablespoon of honey.
Sprinkle 1/4 cup of chopped nuts over the yogurt in each bowl.
If desired, top each serving with fresh fruit or berries of your choice.
Serve immediately or refrigerate until ready to serve. Can be stored in the refrigerator for up to 2 days.

Nutritional Information (per serving):

Calories: Approximately 300 kcal
Protein: 15 g
Fat: 15 g
Carbohydrates: 25 g
Fiber: 3 g
Sugar: 20 g

21. VGT Cottage Cheese and Fruit Bowl

Prep: 5 min | Cook: 0 min | Total: 5 min

Ingredients:

3 cups cottage cheese
3 cups mixed fresh fruit (such as berries, sliced bananas, and diced peaches)
6 tbsp honey or maple syrup
Optional: a sprinkle of cinnamon or granola for topping

Instructions:

Divide the cottage cheese equally among six serving bowls.
Top each bowl with 1/2 cup of the mixed fresh fruit.
Drizzle each bowl with 1 tablespoon of honey or maple syrup.
Optionally, sprinkle cinnamon or granola on top for added flavor and texture.
Serve immediately or refrigerate until ready to serve. The bowls can be stored in the refrigerator for up to 2 days.

Nutritional Information (per serving):

Calories: Approximately 250 kcal
Protein: 20 g
Fat: 6 g
Carbohydrates: 30 g
Fiber: 2 g
Sugar: 25 g

22. VGT Scrambled Eggs with Herbs

Prep: 5 min | Cook: 10 min | Total: 15 min

Ingredients:

12 large eggs
1/4 cup milk
2 tbsp butter
1/4 cup mixed fresh herbs (such as parsley, chives, and basil), finely chopped
Salt and pepper to taste

Instructions:

In a large bowl, whisk together the eggs and milk until well combined. Season with salt and pepper.
Heat butter in a large non-stick skillet over medium heat until melted.
Pour in the egg mixture. Let it sit, without stirring, for 20 seconds.
Gently stir with a spatula, lifting and folding the eggs from the bottom of the pan.
Continue cooking, stirring occasionally, until the eggs are softly set and slightly runny in places, about 3-4 minutes.
Remove from the heat and gently fold in the chopped herbs.
Divide the scrambled eggs among 6 plates. Serve immediately, or let cool and store in the refrigerator for up to 2 days.

Nutritional Information (per serving):

Calories: Approximately 200 kcal
Protein: 14 g
Fat: 15 g
Carbohydrates: 2 g
Fiber: 0 g
Sugar: 1 g

23. VGT Banana and Walnut Pancakes

Prep: 15 min | Cook: 15 min | Total: 30 min

Ingredients:

2 cups whole wheat flour
2 tsp baking powder
1/2 tsp baking soda
1/4 tsp salt
2 ripe bananas, mashed
2 cups almond milk
2 large eggs
2 tbsp honey
1/2 cup walnuts, chopped
Cooking spray or butter for the pan

Instructions:

In a large bowl, mix together the flour, baking powder, baking soda, and salt.

In another bowl, combine the mashed bananas, almond milk, eggs, and honey.

Gradually add the wet ingredients to the dry ingredients, stirring until just combined. Fold in the chopped walnuts.

Heat a non-stick skillet over medium heat and lightly grease with cooking spray or butter.

Pour about 1/4 cup of batter for each pancake onto the skillet. Cook for 2-3 minutes on each side or until golden brown and cooked through.

Serve warm with additional honey or syrup if desired.

Store any leftover pancakes in the refrigerator for up to 2 days.

Nutritional Information (per serving, 2 pancakes):

Calories: Approximately 300 kcal
Protein: 9 g
Fat: 10 g
Carbohydrates: 45 g
Fiber: 6 g
Sugar: 10 g

24. VGT Cheesy Broccoli Breakfast Muffins

Prep: 15 min | Cook: 20 min | Total: 35 min

Ingredients:

2 cups whole wheat flour
1 tbsp baking powder
1/2 tsp salt
1/4 tsp black pepper
1 cup broccoli florets, finely chopped
1 cup cheddar cheese, shredded
1 cup milk
1/4 cup olive oil
2 large eggs
Cooking spray or muffin liners for the pan

Instructions:

Preheat the oven to 375°F (190°C). Prepare a muffin tin with cooking spray or liners.

In a large bowl, whisk together flour, baking powder, salt, and pepper.

Stir in the broccoli and cheddar cheese.

In another bowl, mix together milk, olive oil, and eggs.

Add the wet ingredients to the dry ingredients, stirring until just combined.

Fill each muffin cup about 3/4 full with the batter.

Bake for 20-25 minutes, or until the muffins are golden and a toothpick inserted into the center comes out clean.

Let the muffins cool in the pan for 5 minutes, then transfer to a wire rack.

Serve warm or store in an airtight container in the refrigerator for up to 3 days.

Nutritional Information (per muffin, makes 12):

Calories: Approximately 180 kcal, Protein: 6 g
Fat: 10 g, Carbohydrates: 18 g, Fiber: 2 g, Sugar: 2 g

25. VGT Tomato and Basil Bruschetta

Prep: 10 min | Cook: 5 min | Total: 15 min

Ingredients:

6 large ripe tomatoes, diced
1/4 cup fresh basil leaves, chopped
2 cloves garlic, minced
2 tbsp olive oil
1 tbsp balsamic vinegar
Salt and pepper to taste
1 baguette, sliced and toasted

Instructions:

In a bowl, combine diced tomatoes, chopped basil, minced garlic, olive oil, and balsamic vinegar. Season with salt and pepper to taste. Let the mixture sit for 15 minutes to blend the flavors.
Preheat the oven to 375°F (190°C).
Arrange the baguette slices on a baking sheet and toast in the oven for 5-7 minutes, or until golden and crisp.
Spoon the tomato mixture generously onto each toasted baguette slice.
Serve immediately. Best enjoyed fresh, but the tomato mixture can be stored in the refrigerator for up to 1 day.

Nutritional Information (per serving, 2 slices):

Calories: Approximately 150 kcal
Protein: 3 g
Fat: 5 g
Carbohydrates: 22 g
Fiber: 2 g
Sugar: 3 g

26. VGT Mushroom and Swiss Cheese Frittata

Prep: 10 min | Cook: 20 min | Total: 30 min

Ingredients:

8 large eggs
1/2 cup milk
1 cup Swiss cheese, shredded
2 cups mushrooms, sliced
1 onion, diced
2 tbsp olive oil
Salt and pepper to taste
Fresh parsley, chopped, for garnish

Instructions:

Preheat the oven to 375°F (190°C).
In a large bowl, whisk together eggs, milk, salt, and pepper.
Stir in the shredded Swiss cheese.
In an oven-safe skillet, heat olive oil over medium heat. Sauté onions until translucent, then add mushrooms and cook until they release their moisture and brown slightly.
Pour the egg mixture over the mushrooms and onions. Cook without stirring for about 5 minutes, or until the edges begin to set.
Transfer the skillet to the oven and bake for 15-20 minutes, or until the frittata is set and lightly golden on top.
Remove from the oven, let cool for a few minutes, then garnish with fresh parsley.
Cut into wedges and serve. Store any leftovers in the refrigerator for up to 2 days.

Nutritional Information (per serving, 6 servings total):

Calories: Approximately 250 kcal
Protein: 18 g
Fat: 18 g
Carbohydrates: 5 g
Fiber: 1 g
Sugar: 3 g

27. VGT Baked Spinach and Ricotta Crepes

Prep: 20 min | Cook: 30 min | Total: 50 min

Ingredients:

For the crepes:
1 1/2 cups all-purpose flour
2 cups milk
2 eggs
1 tbsp vegetable oil
Pinch of salt
For the filling:
2 cups ricotta cheese
2 cups spinach, cooked and chopped
1/2 cup Parmesan cheese, grated
Salt and pepper to taste
Nutmeg, a pinch

Instructions:

For the crepes, blend flour, milk, eggs, oil, and salt until smooth. Let the batter rest for 30 minutes.
Heat a non-stick skillet over medium heat. Pour 1/4 cup of batter per crepe and swirl to spread evenly. Cook until lightly golden, then flip and cook the other side. Repeat with remaining batter.
For the filling, mix ricotta, spinach, Parmesan, salt, pepper, and nutmeg.
Place a spoonful of filling on each crepe, roll up, and place in a baking dish.
Bake at 375°F (190°C) for 20 minutes.
Serve hot.
Store any leftovers in the refrigerator for up to 2 days.

Nutritional Information (per serving, 1 crepe):

Calories: Approximately 250 kcal, Protein: 15 g, Fat: 10 g, Carbohydrates: 25 g, Fiber: 2 g, Sugar: 4 g

28. VGT Cinnamon and Apple French Toast

Prep: 10 min | Cook: 10 min | Total: 20 min

Ingredients:

12 slices of whole grain bread
4 eggs
1 cup milk
2 apples, thinly sliced
2 tsp cinnamon
2 tbsp butter
Maple syrup for serving

Instructions:

In a shallow dish, whisk together eggs, milk, and cinnamon.
Melt butter in a large skillet over medium heat.
Dip each bread slice in the egg mixture, ensuring both sides are coated.
Fry the bread slices in the skillet, adding apple slices on top, until golden brown on each side.
Serve with maple syrup.
Store any unused apple slices and egg mixture separately in the refrigerator.

Nutritional Information (per serving, 2 slices):

Calories: Approximately 300 kcal
Protein: 12 g
Fat: 10 g
Carbohydrates: 40 g
Fiber: 5 g
Sugar: 15 g

29. VGT Zucchini and Carrot Fritters

Prep: 15 min | Cook: 15 min | Total: 30 min

Ingredients:

2 cups zucchini, grated
1 cup carrots, grated
1/2 cup all-purpose flour
2 eggs
1/2 tsp garlic powder
Salt and pepper to taste
4 tbsp olive oil
Greek yogurt for serving

Instructions:

Squeeze out excess moisture from the grated zucchini and carrots using a clean kitchen towel.
In a bowl, mix zucchini, carrots, flour, eggs, garlic powder, salt, and pepper.
Heat olive oil in a skillet over medium heat.
Spoon the mixture into the skillet, flattening to form fritters. Cook until golden brown on each side.
Serve with a dollop of Greek yogurt.
Store any leftovers in the refrigerator for up to 2 days.

Nutritional Information (per serving, 2 fritters):

Calories: Approximately 250 kcal
Protein: 8 g
Fat: 15 g
Carbohydrates: 20 g
Fiber: 3 g
Sugar: 5 g

30. VGT Ricotta and Honey Crostini

Prep: 5 min | Cook: 5 min | Total: 10 min

Ingredients:

12 slices of whole grain baguette
1 1/2 cups ricotta cheese
1/4 cup honey
Zest of 1 lemon
1/4 cup walnuts, chopped
Fresh thyme leaves for garnish

Instructions:

Toast the baguette slices until golden brown.
Spread ricotta cheese evenly on each slice.
Drizzle with honey and sprinkle with lemon zest.
Top with chopped walnuts and garnish with thyme leaves.
Serve immediately.
Store any unused ricotta mixture in the refrigerator for up to 2 days.

Nutritional Information (per serving, 1 crostini):

Calories: Approximately 200 kcal
Protein: 8 g
Fat: 10 g
Carbohydrates: 20 g
Fiber: 2 g
Sugar: 6 g

31. VGT Egg and Cheese Bagel Sandwich

Prep: 5 min | Cook: 5 min | Total: 10 min

Ingredients:

6 whole grain bagels, sliced and toasted
6 eggs
6 slices cheddar cheese
2 tbsp butter
Salt and pepper to taste
Fresh spinach leaves (optional)

Instructions:

In a skillet, melt butter over medium heat. Fry eggs to your preferred doneness. Season with salt and pepper.

Place a slice of cheddar cheese on each egg while still in the skillet to melt slightly.

Assemble the sandwich with the cheesy egg and fresh spinach leaves between the bagel slices.

Serve immediately.

Store any leftover bagels separately in the refrigerator.

Nutritional Information (per serving, 1 sandwich):

Calories: Approximately 350 kcal
Protein: 20 g
Fat: 15 g
Carbohydrates: 35 g
Fiber: 5 g
Sugar: 5 g

32. VGT Strawberry and Cream Cheese Scones

Prep: 20 min | Cook: 20 min | Total: 40 min

Ingredients:

2 cups all-purpose flour
1/4 cup sugar
1 tbsp baking powder
1/2 tsp salt
1/2 cup cold butter, cubed
3/4 cup cream cheese, softened
1 cup strawberries, chopped
1/2 cup milk
1 egg, beaten for glaze

Instructions:

Preheat the oven to 400°F (200°C).

In a large bowl, mix flour, sugar, baking powder, and salt.

Cut in the butter until the mixture resembles coarse crumbs.

Stir in cream cheese and strawberries.

Gradually add milk, stirring until a dough forms.

Turn out onto a floured surface and gently knead. Roll out to 1-inch thickness and cut into scone shapes.

Place on a baking sheet, brush with beaten egg, and bake for 15-20 minutes, or until golden brown.

Serve warm.

Store any leftovers in an airtight container for up to 2 days.

Nutritional Information (per serving, 1 scone):

Calories: Approximately 300 kcal
Protein: 6 g
Fat: 16 g
Carbohydrates: 35
Fiber: 1 g
Sugar: 10 g

Fish & Meat Breakfast Recipes

33. Herbed Shrimp and Asparagus Frittata

Prep: 15 min | Cook: 15 min | Total: 30 min

Ingredients:

12 eggs
1/2 cup milk
1 lb shrimp, peeled and deveined
2 cups asparagus, chopped
1/2 cup feta cheese, crumbled
1/4 cup fresh dill, chopped
2 tbsp olive oil
Salt and pepper to taste

Instructions:

Preheat the oven to 375°F (190°C).
In a bowl, whisk together eggs, milk, dill, salt, and pepper.
Heat olive oil in an oven-safe skillet over medium heat. Sauté asparagus until tender.
Add shrimp and cook until pink.
Pour the egg mixture over the shrimp and asparagus. Sprinkle with feta cheese.
Cook until the edges start to set, then transfer to the oven.
Bake for 15-20 minutes or until the frittata is set and lightly golden.
Serve hot or allow to cool and store in the refrigerator for up to 2 days.

Nutritional Information (per serving, 1 slice):

Calories: Approximately 300 kcal, Protein: 30 g
Fat: 18 g, Carbohydrates: 5 g, Fiber: 1 g, Sugar: 3 g

34. Lox and Bagels with Capers

Prep: 10 min | Cook: 0 min | Total: 10 min

Ingredients:

6 plain or everything bagels, halved and toasted
12 oz lox (thinly sliced smoked salmon)
1 cup whipped cream cheese
1/4 cup capers, drained
1 small red onion, thinly sliced
Fresh dill and lemon wedges for garnish

Instructions:

Spread whipped cream cheese on each toasted bagel half.
Arrange lox slices over the cream cheese.
Sprinkle capers and add a few red onion slices on top.
Garnish with fresh dill and serve with lemon wedges on the side.
Serve immediately. Wrap and refrigerate any leftovers for up to 1 day.

Nutritional Information (per serving):

Calories: Approximately 350 kcal
Protein: 22 g
Fat: 10 g
Carbohydrates: 45 g
Fiber: 3 g
Sugar: 7 g

35.   Smoked Salmon and Avocado Omelette

Prep: 10 min | Cook: 10 min | Total: 20 min

Ingredients:

12 large eggs
1/2 cup milk
Salt and pepper to taste
2 avocados, sliced
6 oz smoked salmon, cut into strips
1/2 cup cream cheese, softened
2 tbsp chives, chopped
2 tbsp olive oil

Instructions:

In a bowl, whisk together eggs, milk, salt, and pepper.
Heat 1 tbsp of olive oil in a non-stick skillet over medium heat.
Pour in 1/6 of the egg mixture and cook until the edges begin to set.
Place slices of avocado, smoked salmon, and a dollop of cream cheese on one half of the omelette.
Fold the omelette over the filling and cook until the egg is set.
Repeat the process for the remaining omelettes, using additional olive oil as needed.
Garnish with chopped chives before serving.
Serve immediately or store in the refrigerator for up to 1 day.

Nutritional Information (per serving, 6 servings total):

Calories: Approximately 350 kcal
Protein: 23 g
Fat: 25 g
Carbohydrates: 8 g
Fiber: 4 g
Sugar: 3 g

36.   Shrimp and Grits

Prep: 15 min | Cook: 30 min | Total: 45 min

Ingredients:

1 1/2 cups quick-cooking grits
6 cups water
1/2 cup cheddar cheese, grated
2 tbsp butter
1 lb shrimp, peeled and deveined
1 small onion, diced
1 bell pepper, diced
2 cloves garlic, minced
1/2 tsp smoked paprika
Salt and pepper to taste
2 tbsp olive oil
Fresh parsley for garnish

Instructions:

In a large saucepan, bring water to a boil. Gradually whisk in grits, reduce heat, and simmer, stirring frequently, until thickened (about 5-7 minutes).
Stir in cheddar cheese and butter until melted.
Season with salt and pepper. Keep warm.
Heat olive oil in a skillet over medium heat. Add onion, bell pepper, and garlic, cooking until softened.
Add shrimp, smoked paprika, salt, and pepper. Cook until the shrimp are pink and opaque.
Serve the shrimp mixture over the grits.
Garnish with fresh parsley.
Serve immediately. Store any leftovers in the refrigerator for up to 2 days.

Nutritional Information (per serving, 6 servings total):

Calories: Approximately 350 kcal
Protein: 25 g
Fat: 12 g
Carbohydrates: 35 g
Fiber: 2 g
Sugar: 3 g

37.   Crab and Avocado Toast

Prep: 15 min | Cook: 5 min | Total: 20 min

Ingredients:

6 slices of whole grain bread, toasted
12 oz lump crab meat
2 avocados, mashed
1 tbsp lemon juice
1/4 cup mayonnaise
1 tsp Dijon mustard
1/4 cup red onion, finely chopped
2 tbsp chives, chopped
Salt and pepper to taste
Lemon wedges for serving

Instructions:

In a bowl, mix together mashed avocados and lemon juice. Season with salt and pepper.
Spread the avocado mixture evenly over the toasted bread slices.
In another bowl, combine crab meat, mayonnaise, Dijon mustard, red onion, and chives. Season with salt and pepper to taste.
Top each avocado toast with a generous portion of the crab mixture.
Garnish with more chopped chives.
Serve immediately with lemon wedges on the side. Store any leftover crab mixture in the refrigerator for up to 1 day.

Nutritional Information (per serving, 6 servings total):

Calories: Approximately 300 kcal
Protein: 20 g
Fat: 15 g
Carbohydrates: 25 g
Fiber: 5 g
Sugar: 4 g

38.   Ham and Egg English Muffin

Prep: 5 min | Cook: 5 min | Total: 10 min

Ingredients:

6 English muffins, split and toasted
6 eggs
6 slices of ham
6 slices of cheddar cheese
Salt and pepper to taste
Butter for cooking and spreading

Instructions:

Lightly butter each half of the English muffins and set aside.
Heat a non-stick skillet over medium heat. Add a little butter for cooking.
Crack an egg into the skillet, season with salt and pepper, and cook to your preference. Repeat for the remaining eggs.
Assemble the sandwiches by placing a slice of ham and a slice of cheese on each muffin bottom.
Top with a cooked egg and the other muffin half.
Serve immediately. If storing, wrap each sandwich individually and refrigerate for up to 1 day.

Nutritional Information (per sandwich):

Calories: Approximately 350 kcal
Protein: 25 g
Fat: 15 g
Carbohydrates: 30 g
Fiber: 2 g
Sugar: 3 g

39. Bacon and Spinach Quiche

Prep: 15 min | Cook: 35 min | Total: 50 min

Ingredients:

1 pre-made pie crust
6 large eggs
1 cup heavy cream
1 cup spinach, chopped
6 slices bacon, cooked and crumbled
1/2 cup cheddar cheese, shredded
1/4 cup Parmesan cheese, grated
Salt and pepper to taste
1/2 tsp nutmeg

Instructions:

Preheat the oven to 375°F (190°C). Place the pie crust in a 9-inch pie dish.
In a skillet, cook the bacon until crisp. Drain on paper towels, then crumble.
In the same skillet, sauté spinach until wilted. Remove from heat.
In a bowl, whisk together eggs, heavy cream, salt, pepper, and nutmeg.
Layer the crumbled bacon, cooked spinach, and cheddar cheese in the pie crust.
Pour the egg mixture over the fillings. Sprinkle the top with grated Parmesan cheese.
Bake for 35-40 minutes, or until the quiche is set and lightly golden on top.
Allow to cool for a few minutes before slicing and serving.
Store any leftovers in the refrigerator for up to 2 days.

Nutritional Information (per serving, 6 servings total):

Calories: Approximately 350 kcal
Protein: 14 g
Fat: 25 g
Carbohydrates: 15 g
Fiber: 1 g
Sugar: 2 g

40. Turkey Sausage and Vegetable Skillet

Prep: 15 min | Cook: 15 min | Total: 30 min

Ingredients:

1 lb turkey sausage, casings removed
1 bell pepper, diced
1 onion, diced
2 cups baby spinach
1 cup cherry tomatoes, halved
1 tsp garlic powder
Salt and pepper to taste
2 tbsp olive oil

Instructions:

Heat olive oil in a large skillet over medium heat. Add the turkey sausage, breaking it apart with a spatula. Cook until browned.
Add diced bell pepper and onion to the skillet. Cook until the vegetables are tender.
Stir in baby spinach and cherry tomatoes, cooking until the spinach is wilted.
Season with garlic powder, salt, and pepper.
Serve hot. Store any leftovers in the refrigerator for up to 2 days.

Nutritional Information (per serving, 6 servings total):

Calories: Approximately 250 kcal
Protein: 20 g
Fat: 15 g
Carbohydrates: 10 g
Fiber: 2 g
Sugar: 4 g

41. Breakfast Steak and Eggs

Prep: 5 min | Cook: 10 min | Total: 15 min

Ingredients:

1 lb sirloin steak, cut into 6 portions
6 large eggs
Salt and pepper to taste
1 tbsp olive oil
1 tbsp butter
Fresh parsley, chopped, for garnish

Instructions:

Season the steak portions with salt and pepper. Heat olive oil in a large skillet over medium-high heat. Add the steak and cook to your desired level of doneness, about 3-4 minutes per side for medium-rare. Remove from the skillet and keep warm.
In the same skillet, melt the butter. Crack the eggs into the skillet and cook to your preference (fried, scrambled, or over-easy).
Serve each steak portion with a cooked egg on top.
Garnish with chopped parsley.
Serve immediately. Store any leftover steak and eggs in the refrigerator for up to 2 days.

Nutritional Information (per serving):

Calories: Approximately 350 kcal
Protein: 35 g
Fat: 20 g
Carbohydrates: 1 g
Fiber: 0 g
Sugar: 0 g

42. Chicken and Waffle Sandwich

Prep: 20 min | Cook: 20 min | Total: 40 min

Ingredients:

6 waffles, toasted
6 small chicken breasts, cooked and sliced
1/2 cup maple syrup
Salt and pepper to taste
6 lettuce leaves
6 tomato slices
Butter for toasting waffles

Instructions:

Toast the waffles and butter them lightly.
Season the cooked chicken breast slices with salt and pepper.
Assemble the sandwiches by placing a lettuce leaf and a tomato slice on a waffle.
Add a portion of chicken and drizzle with maple syrup.
Top with another waffle.
Serve immediately. If storing, keep the chicken and waffles separate and assemble just before serving.

Nutritional Information (per sandwich):

Calories: Approximately 350 kcal
Protein: 30 g
Fat: 8 g
Carbohydrates: 40 g
Fiber: 3 g
Sugar: 15 g

43. Biscuit with Sausage Gravy

Prep: 20 min | Cook: 25 min | Total: 45 min

Ingredients:

For the Biscuits:
2 cups all-purpose flour
1 tbsp baking powder
1/2 tsp salt
1/2 cup unsalted butter, cold and cubed
3/4 cup milk
For the Sausage Gravy:
1 lb pork breakfast sausage
3 tbsp butter
1/4 cup all-purpose flour
2 cups milk
Salt and pepper to taste

Instructions:

Make Biscuits: Preheat the oven to 425°F (220°C). In a bowl, combine flour, baking powder, and salt. Cut in the butter until the mixture resembles coarse crumbs. Gradually add milk, stirring until a soft dough forms. Turn out onto a floured surface and knead gently. Roll out and cut into biscuits. Bake for 12-15 minutes.
Make Sausage Gravy: Cook the sausage in a skillet, breaking it into crumbles. Remove sausage and set aside. In the same skillet, melt butter, whisk in flour, and gradually add milk. Cook until thickened. Add cooked sausage, salt, and pepper.
Split the biscuits in half and spoon gravy over them.
Serve immediately. Store any leftover biscuits and gravy separately in the refrigerator for up to 2 days.

Nutritional Information (per serving, 6 servings total):

Calories: Approximately 350 kcal, Protein: 15 g
Fat: 20 g, Carbohydrates: 30 g, Fiber: 1 g, Sugar: 5 g

44. Sausage and Cheese Breakfast Casserole

Prep: 20 min | Cook: 40 min | Total: 1 hr

Ingredients:

1 lb breakfast sausage
6 cups bread, cubed
2 cups cheddar cheese, shredded
10 eggs
2 cups milk
1 tsp mustard powder
Salt and pepper to taste

Instructions:

Preheat the oven to 350°F (175°C). Grease a large baking dish.
Cook sausage until browned. Drain and set aside.
Layer bread cubes, cooked sausage, and cheese in the baking dish.
In a bowl, whisk together eggs, milk, mustard powder, salt, and pepper.
Pour the egg mixture over the bread, sausage, and cheese.
Bake for 45-50 minutes, or until set and golden brown.
Serve hot.
Store leftovers in the refrigerator for up to 3 days.

Nutritional Information (per serving):

Calories: Approximately 350 kcal
Protein: 25 g
Fat: 20 g
Carbohydrates: 20 g
Fiber: 2 g
Sugar: 5 g

45.   Corned Beef Hash with Eggs

Prep: 15 min | Cook: 20 min | Total: 35 min

Ingredients:

3 cups cooked corned beef, diced
4 large potatoes, diced
1 large onion, diced
6 eggs
4 tbsp olive oil
Salt and pepper to taste
Fresh parsley for garnish

Instructions:

Heat 2 tablespoons of olive oil in a large skillet over medium heat. Add diced potatoes and cook until golden and crispy, about 10-15 minutes. Season with salt and pepper.
Add the remaining olive oil and diced onion to the skillet. Cook until the onion is translucent.
Add the cooked corned beef to the skillet and mix with the potatoes and onions. Cook for another 5 minutes.
Make six wells in the hash and crack an egg into each well. Cover the skillet and cook until the eggs are set to your desired doneness.
Garnish with fresh parsley before serving.
Store any leftovers in the refrigerator for up to 2 days.

Nutritional Information (per serving):

Calories: Approximately 350 kcal
Protein: 20 g
Fat: 22 g
Carbohydrates: 20 g
Fiber: 2 g
Sugar: 2 g

46.   Spicy Turkey Breakfast Patties

Prep: 15 min | Cook: 10 min | Total: 25 min

Ingredients:

1 1/2 pounds ground turkey
1 small apple, finely grated
1/4 cup green onions, finely chopped
2 cloves garlic, minced
1 tablespoon fresh sage, minced
1/2 teaspoon cayenne pepper (adjust to taste)
Salt and pepper, to taste
1 tablespoon olive oil for cooking

Instructions:

In a large bowl, combine the ground turkey, grated apple, green onions, garlic, sage, cayenne pepper, salt, and pepper. Mix until well combined.
Form the mixture into 12 small patties.
Heat olive oil in a large skillet over medium heat. Cook patties for 4-5 minutes on each side until golden and cooked through.
Serve immediately or let cool and store in the refrigerator or freezer for later use.

Nutritional Information per serving:

Calories approximate: 250
Protein: 30g
Fat: 12g
Carbohydrates: 4g
Fiber: 1g
Sugar: 5 g

47. Breakfast BLT Sandwich

Prep: 10 min | Cook: 10 min | Total: 20 min

Ingredients:

12 slices of whole-grain bread
12 slices of bacon, cooked
1 large tomato, sliced
6 lettuce leaves
6 eggs, fried
Mayonnaise for spreading
Salt and pepper to taste

Instructions:

Toast the bread slices until golden brown.
Spread mayonnaise on one side of each bread slice.
Layer bacon, lettuce, tomato slices, and a fried egg on half of the bread slices. Season with salt and pepper.
Top with the remaining bread slices to form sandwiches.
Serve immediately.
Store any unused ingredients separately in the refrigerator.

Nutritional Information (per serving, 1 sandwich):

Calories: Approximately 350 kcal
Protein: 20 g
Fat: 18 g
Carbohydrates: 30 g
Fiber: 5 g
Sugar: 5 g

Vegan Snack Recipes

48. VGN Roasted Chickpeas

Prep: 5 min | Cook: 30 min | Total: 35 min

Ingredients:

3 cans (15 oz each) chickpeas, drained, rinsed, and patted dry
3 tbsp olive oil
1 1/2 tsp smoked paprika
1 1/2 tsp ground cumin
Salt to taste

Instructions:

Preheat the oven to 400°F (200°C).
In a bowl, toss the chickpeas with olive oil, smoked paprika, cumin, and salt.
Spread the chickpeas in a single layer on a baking sheet.
Roast for 25-30 minutes, stirring occasionally, until crispy and golden.
Let them cool before serving. Store in an airtight container for up to a week.

Nutritional Information (per serving):

Calories: Approximately 150 kcal
Protein: 5 g
Fat: 7 g
Carbohydrates: 15 g
Fiber: 4 g
Sugar: 0 g

49. VGN Guacamole and Tortilla Chips

Prep: 10 min | Cook: 0 min | Total: 10 min

Ingredients:

3 ripe avocados, mashed
Juice of 1 lime
1/2 red onion, finely chopped
1 tomato, diced
1/4 cup cilantro, chopped
Salt and pepper to taste
6 servings of whole grain tortilla chips

Instructions:

In a bowl, combine mashed avocados, lime juice, red onion, tomato, and cilantro. Season with salt and pepper.
Adjust the seasoning as needed and mix until well combined.
Serve the guacamole with tortilla chips.
Store any leftover guacamole in an airtight container with plastic wrap pressed directly onto the surface of the guacamole to prevent browning. Keep refrigerated and consume within 2 days.

Nutritional Information (per serving, guacamole only):

Calories: Approximately 150 kcal
Protein: 2 g
Fat: 12 g
Carbohydrates: 10 g
Fiber: 7 g
Sugar: 1 g

50. VGN Vegan Protein Bars

Prep: 15 min | Cook: 0 min (Refrigerate to set) | Total: 15 min + refrigeration

Ingredients:

2 cups rolled oats
1 cup peanut or almond butter
1/2 cup maple syrup
1/2 cup vegan protein powder
1/4 cup chia seeds
1/4 cup dark chocolate chips (vegan)
1/2 tsp vanilla extract

Instructions:

Line an 8x8 inch baking pan with parchment paper.
In a large bowl, mix together oats, protein powder, and chia seeds.
In a separate bowl, combine peanut or almond butter, maple syrup, and vanilla extract.
Mix the wet ingredients into the dry ingredients until well combined. Fold in the chocolate chips.
Press the mixture firmly into the prepared pan.
Freeze for 1-2 hours until firm. Cut into bars.
Store in an airtight container in the refrigerator for up to a week.

Nutritional Information (per bar, makes 12):

Calories: Approximately 250 kcal
Protein: 10 g
Fat: 12 g
Carbohydrates: 25 g
Fiber: 4 g
Sugar: 10 g

51.   VGN Spiced Nuts Mix

Prep: 5 min | Cook: 10 min | Total: 15 min

Ingredients:

2 cups mixed nuts (almonds, walnuts, pecans)
1 tbsp olive oil
1 tsp smoked paprika
1/2 tsp ground cumin
1/2 tsp chili powder
1/2 tsp garlic powder
Salt to taste

Instructions:

Preheat the oven to 350°F (175°C).
In a bowl, mix the nuts with olive oil, smoked paprika, cumin, chili powder, garlic powder, and salt.
Spread the nuts on a baking sheet in a single layer.
Roast for 10-15 minutes, stirring occasionally, until the nuts are lightly toasted.
Allow cooling before serving. Store in an airtight container for up to 2 weeks.

Nutritional Information (per serving, 1/4 cup):

Calories: Approximately 200 kcal
Protein: 5 g
Fat: 18 g
Carbohydrates: 6 g
Fiber: 3 g
Sugar: 1 g

52.   VGN Fruit Leather

Prep: 15 min | Cook: 3-4 hours | Total: 3-4 hours 15 min

Ingredients:

4 cups mixed berries (strawberries, raspberries, blueberries)
2 tbsp maple syrup
Juice of 1 lemon

Instructions:

Preheat the oven to 170°F (75°C). Line a baking sheet with parchment paper.
In a blender, puree the berries, maple syrup, and lemon juice until smooth.
Pour the mixture onto the prepared baking sheet and spread evenly with a spatula.
Bake for 3-4 hours, or until the fruit leather is dry to the touch but still pliable.
Remove from the oven and let cool. Cut into strips and roll up.
Store in an airtight container for up to a week.

Nutritional Information (per serving, 1 strip):

Calories: Approximately 50 kcal
Protein: 0 g,
Fat: 0 g
Carbohydrates: 12 g
Fiber: 2 g
ugar: 10 g

53. VGN Edamame with Sea Salt

Prep: 0 min | Cook: 5 min | Total: 5 min

Ingredients:

3 cups frozen edamame in the pod
1 tbsp sea salt

Instructions:

Bring a pot of water to a boil. Add the edamame and cook for 5 minutes or until tender.
Drain the edamame and sprinkle with sea salt.
Serve warm or at room temperature. Store in an airtight container in the refrigerator for up to 3 days.

Nutritional Information (per serving, 1/2 cup):

Calories: Approximately 120 kcal
Protein: 11 g
Fat: 5 g
Carbohydrates: 9 g
Fiber: 4 g
Sugar: 2 g

54. VGN Carrot and Cucumber Sticks with Hummus

Prep: 10 min | Cook: 0 min | Total: 10 min

Ingredients:

3 large carrots, peeled and cut into sticks
3 cucumbers, cut into sticks
2 cups hummus (store-bought or homemade)

Instructions:

Arrange carrot and cucumber sticks on a serving platter.
Serve with hummus for dipping.
Store any leftover vegetables and hummus in separate airtight containers in the refrigerator for up to 3 days.

Nutritional Information (per serving, including hummus):

Calories: Approximately 150 kcal
Protein: 5 g
Fat: 8 g
Carbohydrates: 15 g
Fiber: 4 g
Sugar: 5 g

55. VGN Banana Muffins

Prep: 15 min | Cook: 25 min | Total: 40 min

Ingredients:

2 cups whole wheat flour
1 tsp baking soda
1/2 tsp salt
1/2 cup unsweetened applesauce
3/4 cup maple syrup
4 ripe bananas, mashed
1/4 cup almond milk
1 tsp vanilla extract

Instructions:

Preheat the oven to 350°F (175°C). Line a muffin tin with paper liners.

In a large bowl, mix together flour, baking soda, and salt.

In another bowl, combine applesauce, maple syrup, mashed bananas, almond milk, and vanilla extract.

Add the wet ingredients to the dry ingredients, mixing until just combined.

Pour the batter into the muffin tin, filling each cup about 3/4 full.

Bake for 20-25 minutes, or until a toothpick inserted into the center comes out clean.

Cool in the tin for 5 minutes, then transfer to a wire rack to cool completely.

Store in an airtight container for up to 5 days.

Nutritional Information (per muffin, makes 12):

Calories: Approximately 180 kcal
Protein: 3 g
Fat: 1 g
Carbohydrates: 40 g
Fiber: 4 g
Sugar: 15 g

56. VGN Peanut Butter and Jelly Sandwich Squares

Prep: 10 min | Cook: 0 min | Total: 10 min

Ingredients:

12 slices whole grain bread
3/4 cup peanut butter
3/4 cup jelly or jam (sugar-free or low sugar)

Instructions:

Spread peanut butter on six slices of bread.

Spread jelly or jam on the other six slices of bread.

Sandwich the slices together and cut each into four squares.

Serve immediately, or store in an airtight container in the refrigerator for up to 3 days.

Nutritional Information (per square):

Calories: Approximately 100 kcal
Protein: 3 g
Fat: 4 g
Carbohydrates: 13 g
Fiber: 2 g
Sugar: 5 g (varies based on the type of jelly/jam used)

57.   VGN Sweet Potato Fries

Prep: 10 min | Cook: 25 min | Total: 35 min

Ingredients:

3 large sweet potatoes, peeled and cut into fries
3 tbsp olive oil
1 tsp paprika
Salt and pepper to taste

Instructions:

Preheat the oven to 425°F (220°C). Line a baking sheet with parchment paper.
Toss the sweet potato fries with olive oil, paprika, salt, and pepper.
Spread the fries in a single layer on the baking sheet.
Bake for 25-30 minutes, turning halfway through, until crispy and golden.
Serve immediately, or let cool and store in an airtight container in the refrigerator for up to 3 days. Reheat in the oven to retain crispiness.

Nutritional Information (per serving):

Calories: Approximately 200 kcal
Protein: 2 g
Fat: 10 g
Carbohydrates: 27 g
Fiber: 4 g

Vegetarian Snack Recipes

58.   VGT Greek Yogurt and Granola Cups

Prep: 10 min | Cook: 0 min | Total: 10 min

Ingredients:

2 cups Greek yogurt
1 cup granola
1 cup mixed berries (strawberries, blueberries, raspberries)
2 tbsp honey

Instructions:

In six small cups or bowls, layer the Greek yogurt and granola.
Top each cup with a mix of berries.
Drizzle honey over each serving.
Serve immediately or refrigerate for up to 2 days. Stir before eating if refrigerated.

Nutritional Information (per serving):

Calories: Approximately 200 kcal
Protein: 10 g
Fat: 5 g
Carbohydrates: 30 g
Fiber: 3 g
Sugar: 20 g

59. VGT Caprese Salad Skewers

Prep: 15 min | Cook: 0 min | Total: 15 min

Ingredients:

12 cherry tomatoes
12 mini mozzarella balls
12 fresh basil leaves
2 tbsp olive oil
1 tbsp balsamic glaze
Salt and pepper to taste

Instructions:

On small skewers, alternate cherry tomatoes, mini mozzarella balls, and basil leaves.
Arrange the skewers on a platter.
Drizzle with olive oil and balsamic glaze.
Season with salt and pepper to taste.
Serve immediately or refrigerate for up to 1 day.

Nutritional Information (per skewer):

Calories: Approximately 50 kcal
Protein: 3 g
Fat: 4 g
Carbohydrates: 2 g
Fiber: 0.5 g
Sugar: 1 g

60. VGT Baked Mozzarella Sticks

Prep: 10 min | Cook: 10 min | Total: 20 min + refrigeration

Ingredients:

12 mozzarella string cheese sticks
1/2 cup flour
2 large eggs, beaten
1 cup breadcrumbs
1 tsp Italian seasoning
1/2 tsp garlic powder
Marinara sauce for dipping

Instructions:

Preheat the oven to 400°F (200°C). Line a baking sheet with parchment paper.
Cut the mozzarella sticks in half to make 24 pieces.
Dredge each piece in flour, dip in beaten egg, then coat with breadcrumbs mixed with Italian seasoning and garlic powder.
Place on the baking sheet and freeze for 15 minutes.
Bake for 10-12 minutes or until golden brown.
Serve with marinara sauce for dipping. Store any leftovers in the refrigerator for up to 2 days.

Nutritional Information (per serving, 4 sticks):

Calories: Approximately 300 kcal
Protein: 18 g
Fat: 15 g
Carbohydrates: 20 g
Fiber: 1 g
Sugar: 3 g

61. VGT Fruit and Cheese Platter

Prep: 15 min | Cook: 0 min | Total: 15 min

Ingredients:

Assorted cheeses (Brie, Cheddar, Gouda, etc.)
Assorted fresh fruits (grapes, apple slices, pear slices)
Crackers and/or bread slices
Nuts and dried fruits
Honey or fruit preserves for drizzling

Instructions:

Arrange a selection of cheeses, fresh fruits, crackers/bread, nuts, and dried fruits on a large platter.
Drizzle honey or fruit preserves over the cheese for added flavor.
Serve as a snack platter. This dish is best enjoyed fresh but can be refrigerated for a few hours if covered.

Nutritional Information: Varies based on the ingredients used.

Just to give you an idea.
Calories: Approximately 115 calories per 1 ounce

62. VGT Spinach and Artichoke Dip

Prep: 10 min | Cook: 25 min | Total: 35 min

Ingredients:

1 cup cooked and chopped spinach
1 can (14 oz) artichoke hearts, drained and chopped
1 cup cream cheese
1/2 cup sour cream
1/2 cup grated Parmesan cheese
1/2 tsp garlic powder
Salt and pepper to taste

Instructions:

Preheat the oven to 375°F (190°C).
In a bowl, combine spinach, artichoke hearts, cream cheese, sour cream, Parmesan cheese, garlic powder, salt, and pepper.
Transfer the mixture to a baking dish and bake for 20-25 minutes until bubbly and golden on top.
Serve warm with crackers or bread. Store any leftovers in the refrigerator for up to 3 days.

Nutritional Information (per serving, 1/4 cup):

Calories: Approximately 150 kcal
Protein: 5 g
Fat: 12 g
Carbohydrates: 5 g
Fiber: 1 g
Sugar: 2 g

63. VGT Stuffed Cherry Tomatoes

Prep: 20 min | Cook: 0 min | Total: 20 min

Ingredients:

24 cherry tomatoes
1 cup goat cheese, softened
1 tbsp fresh basil, finely chopped
1 tbsp olive oil
Salt and pepper to taste

Instructions:

Slice the tops off the cherry tomatoes and scoop out the insides.
In a bowl, mix together goat cheese, basil, olive oil, salt, and pepper.
Fill each tomato with the goat cheese mixture.
Serve immediately or refrigerate for up to 1 day.

Nutritional Information (per tomato):

Calories: Approximately 30 kcal
Protein: 1 g
Fat: 2 g
Carbohydrates: 1 g
Fiber: 0 g
Sugar: 1 g

64. VGT Cheesy Garlic Bread

Prep: 5 min | Cook: 10 min | Total: 15 min

Ingredients:

1 baguette, sliced in half lengthwise
1/2 cup butter, softened
3 cloves garlic, minced
1 cup shredded mozzarella cheese
2 tbsp grated Parmesan cheese
1 tbsp chopped fresh parsley
Salt and pepper to taste

Instructions:

Preheat the oven to 400°F (200°C).
In a bowl, mix together butter, garlic, parsley, salt, and pepper.
Spread the garlic butter evenly over the cut sides of the baguette.
Sprinkle with mozzarella and Parmesan cheeses.
Bake for 10-12 minutes, or until the cheese is melted and bubbly.
Slice and serve warm. Store any leftovers in an airtight container in the refrigerator for up to 2 days.

Nutritional Information (per serving, 1 slice):

Calories: Approximately 200 kcal
Protein: 6 g
Fat: 12 g
Carbohydrates: 15 g
Fiber: 1 g
Sugar: 1 g

65. VGT Veggie and Hummus Roll-Ups

Prep: 15 min | Cook: 0 min | Total: 15 min

Ingredients:

6 large tortillas
1 1/2 cups hummus
1 cucumber, thinly sliced
1 bell pepper, thinly sliced
1 carrot, grated
1 cup spinach leaves
Salt and pepper to taste

Instructions:

Spread hummus evenly over each tortilla.
Arrange cucumber, bell pepper, carrot, and spinach on top of the hummus.
Season with salt and pepper.
Roll up the tortillas tightly and slice into 1-inch pieces.
Serve immediately or store in the refrigerator for up to 1 day.

Nutritional Information (per roll-up):

Calories: Approximately 150 kcal
Protein: 5 g
Fat: 5 g
Carbohydrates: 20 g
Fiber: 3 g
Sugar: 2 g

66. VGT Pesto and Cheese Stuffed Mini Peppers

Prep: 15 min | Cook: 10 min | Total: 25 min

Ingredients:

12 mini bell peppers, halved and seeded
1/2 cup pesto sauce
1/2 cup goat cheese or cream cheese
1/4 cup pine nuts (optional)

Instructions:

Preheat the oven to 375°F (190°C).
Fill each pepper half with a teaspoon of pesto sauce and top with goat cheese or cream cheese. Sprinkle with pine nuts if using.
Bake for 10-15 minutes or until the peppers are tender and the cheese is slightly golden.
Serve warm. Store any leftovers in the refrigerator for up to 2 days.

Nutritional Information (per stuffed pepper half):

Calories: Approximately 50 kcal
Protein: 2 g
Fat: 4 g
Carbohydrates: 2 g
Fiber: 1 g
Sugar: 1 g

67. VGT Cucumber Sandwiches

Prep: 15 min | Cook: 0 min | Total: 15 min

Ingredients:

1 loaf of whole grain bread, sliced
1/2 cup cream cheese, softened
1 cucumber, thinly sliced
2 tbsp fresh dill, chopped
Salt and pepper to taste

Instructions:

Spread cream cheese on half of the bread slices.
Place cucumber slices on top of the cream cheese. Sprinkle with dill, salt, and pepper.
Top with the remaining bread slices to make sandwiches.
Cut each sandwich into quarters and serve.
Store any leftovers in the refrigerator for up to 1 day.

Nutritional Information (per sandwich quarter):

Calories: Approximately 100 kcal
Protein: 3 g
Fat: 4 g
Carbohydrates: 12 g
Fiber: 2 g
Sugar: 2 g

Meat & Fish Snack Recipes

68. Turkey and Cheese Roll-Ups

Prep: 10 min | Cook: 0 min | Total: 10 min

Ingredients:

12 slices of turkey breast (deli-style)
6 slices of Swiss cheese, halved
1/2 cup mixed greens or spinach leaves
2 tbsp mustard or mayonnaise
Salt and pepper to taste

Instructions:

Lay out the turkey slices and spread a thin layer of mustard or mayonnaise on each.
Place a half slice of cheese and some greens on each turkey slice.
Roll up the turkey slices tightly.
Serve immediately or refrigerate for up to 2 days.

Nutritional Information (per roll-up, makes 12):

Calories: Approximately 70 kcal
Protein: 10 g
Fat: 3 g
Carbohydrates: 1 g
Fiber: 0 g
Sugar: 1 g

69. Smoked Salmon and Cucumber Bites

Prep: 15 min | Cook: 0 min | Total: 15 min

Ingredients:

1 cucumber, sliced into rounds
6 oz smoked salmon, cut into bite-sized pieces
1/2 cup cream cheese, softened
Fresh dill for garnish

Instructions:

Spread a small amount of cream cheese on each cucumber round.
Top with a piece of smoked salmon.
Garnish with fresh dill.
Serve immediately or refrigerate for up to 1 day.

Nutritional Information (per bite, makes 24):

Calories: Approximately 30 kcal
Protein: 3 g
Fat: 2 g
Carbohydrates: 1 g
Fiber: 0 g
Sugar: 1 g

70. Chicken Lettuce Wraps

Prep: 15 min | Cook: 10 min | Total: 25 min

Ingredients:

2 cups cooked chicken, shredded
1 bell pepper, diced
1/2 onion, diced
1 tbsp soy sauce
1 tsp sesame oil
1 head iceberg lettuce, leaves separated
Optional toppings: shredded carrots, bean sprouts, chopped peanuts

Instructions:

In a skillet, sauté bell pepper and onion until soft. Add chicken, soy sauce, and sesame oil. Cook until heated through.
Spoon the chicken mixture into lettuce leaves.
Add optional toppings as desired.
Serve immediately. Best enjoyed fresh. Sauce can be stored in the fridge for up to 2 days

Nutritional Information (per wrap, makes 12):

Calories: Approximately 60 kcal
Protein: 8 g
Fat: 2 g
Carbohydrates: 3 g
Fiber: 1 g
Sugar: 1 g

71.   Mini Meatballs with Marinara Sauce

Prep: 20 min | Cook: 20 min | Total: 40 min

Ingredients:

1 lb ground beef or turkey
1/4 cup breadcrumbs
1 egg
1 tsp garlic powder
1 tsp Italian seasoning
Salt and pepper to taste
1 cup marinara sauce for dipping

Instructions:

Preheat the oven to 375°F (190°C). Line a baking sheet with parchment paper.
In a bowl, mix together ground meat, breadcrumbs, egg, garlic powder, Italian seasoning, salt, and pepper.
Form the mixture into small meatballs and place them on the baking sheet.
Bake for 15-20 minutes, or until cooked through.
Serve with marinara sauce for dipping. Store any leftovers in the refrigerator for up to 3 days.

Nutritional Information (per serving, 4 meatballs):

Calories: Approximately 200 kcal
Protein: 20 g
Fat: 10 g
Carbohydrates: 8 g
Fiber: 1 g
Sugar: 2 g

72.   Tuna Salad Stuffed Avocados

Prep: 10 min | Cook: 0 min | Total: 10 min

Ingredients:

2 cans (5 oz each) tuna, drained
1/4 cup mayonnaise
1 celery stalk, finely chopped
1 tbsp lemon juice
Salt and pepper to taste
3 avocados, halved and pitted

Instructions:

In a bowl, mix together tuna, mayonnaise, celery, lemon juice, salt, and pepper.
Spoon the tuna salad into the avocado halves.
Serve immediately or refrigerate for up to 1 day.

Nutritional Information (per stuffed avocado half):

Calories: Approximately 300 kcal
Protein: 15 g
Fat: 25 g
Carbohydrates: 9 g
Fiber: 7 g
Sugar: 1 g

73.   Bacon-Wrapped Dates

Prep: 10 min | Cook: 15 min | Total: 25 min

Ingredients:

24 dates, pitted
12 slices of bacon, halved
Optional: goat cheese or almonds for stuffing

Instructions:

Preheat the oven to 375°F (190°C). Line a baking sheet with parchment paper.
If using, stuff each date with a small amount of goat cheese or an almond.
Wrap each date with a half slice of bacon and secure with a toothpick.
Place on the baking sheet and bake for 15-20 minutes, or until the bacon is crispy.
Serve warm. Store any leftovers in the refrigerator for up to 2 days.

Nutritional Information (per bacon-wrapped date):

Calories: Approximately 70 kcal
Protein: 2 g
Fat: 4 g
Carbohydrates: 7 g
Fiber: 1 g
Sugar: 5 g

74.   Shrimp Ceviche

Prep: 20 min | Cook: 0 min (Marinate) | Total: 20 min + marinating time

Ingredients:

1 lb cooked shrimp, chopped
1/2 red onion, finely chopped
1 cucumber, peeled and diced
1/2 cup fresh cilantro, chopped
Juice of 2 limes
1 avocado, diced
Salt and pepper to taste
Chilies or rocoto pepper (very hot)

Instructions:

In a bowl, combine shrimp, red onion, cucumber, cilantro, and lime juice and avocado. Mix well.
Season with salt, pepper and chili pepper
Gently fold in the avocado.
Refrigerate for at least 30 minutes to marinate
Serve chilled.
Store any leftovers in the refrigerator for up to 2 days.

Nutritional Information (per serving, 6 servings total):

Calories: Approximately 150 kcal
Protein: 20 g
Fat: 6 g
Carbohydrates: 5 g
Fiber: 2 g
Sugar: 1 g

75. Prosciutto-Wrapped Melon

Prep: 10 min | Cook: 0 min | Total: 10 min

Ingredients:

1 cantaloupe, cut into wedges or balls
12 slices prosciutto

Instructions:

Wrap each piece of cantaloupe with a slice of prosciutto.
Secure with a toothpick if necessary.
Arrange on a platter and serve immediately.
Best enjoyed fresh.
Store in the fridge separate up to 3 days.

Nutritional Information (per serving, 2 wrapped pieces):

Calories: Approximately 80 kcal
Protein: 6 g
Fat: 3 g
Carbohydrates: 8 g
Fiber: 1 g
Sugar: 7 g

76. Mini Chicken and Waffle Sliders

Prep: 20 min | Cook: 30 min | Total: 50 min

Ingredients:

12 mini waffles, toasted
12 small cooked chicken tenders
Maple syrup for drizzling
Optional toppings: hot sauce, honey mustard

Instructions:

Place a chicken tender on each mini waffle.
Drizzle with maple syrup and add any optional toppings.
Top with another mini waffle to make a slider.
Serve immediately.

Nutritional Information (per slider):

Calories: Approximately 150 kcal
Protein: 10 g
Fat: 6 g
Carbohydrates: 15 g
Fiber: 1 g
Sugar: 5 g

77. Ham and Swiss Cheese Pinwheels

Prep: 15 min | Cook: 0 min | Total: 15 min

Ingredients:

6 large tortillas
12 slices of ham
6 slices of Swiss cheese
1/4 cup Dijon mustard
1/4 cup light mayonnaise
1 cup spinach leaves

Instructions:

Spread Dijon mustard and mayonnaise evenly over each tortilla.
Layer ham slices and Swiss cheese on top, followed by a layer of spinach leaves.
Roll up the tortillas tightly and slice into 1-inch pinwheels.
Serve immediately or refrigerate until ready to serve.

Nutritional Information (per serving, 2-3 pinwheels):

Calories: Approximately 200 kcal
Protein: 15 g
Fat: 8 g
Carbohydrates: 15 g
Fiber: 2 g
Sugar: 2 g

Vegan Salad Recipes

78. VGN Mixed Greens with Balsamic Vinaigrette

Prep: 10 min | Cook: 0 min | Total: 10 min

Ingredients:

6 cups mixed greens (like spinach, arugula, and lettuce)
1 cucumber, sliced
1/2 red onion, thinly sliced
1 cup cherry tomatoes, halved
For the Vinaigrette:
1/4 cup balsamic vinegar
1/2 cup olive oil
1 tsp Dijon mustard
1 garlic clove, minced
Salt and pepper to taste

Instructions:

In a large bowl, combine mixed greens, cucumber, red onion, and cherry tomatoes.
In a small jar, mix together balsamic vinegar, olive oil, Dijon mustard, minced garlic, salt, and pepper. Shake well to emulsify.
Drizzle the vinaigrette over the salad just before serving and toss gently.
Serve immediately or store the salad and dressing separately in the refrigerator for up to 2 days.

Nutritional Information (per serving):

Calories: Approximately 200 kcal
Protein: 2 g, Fat: 18 g
Carbohydrates: 8 g
Fiber: 2 g, Sugar: 4 g

79. VGN Quinoa and Black Bean Salad

Prep: 15 min | Cook: 15 min (Quinoa) | Total: 30 min

Ingredients:

1 1/2 cups quinoa, cooked and cooled
1 can (15 oz) black beans, drained and rinsed
1 red bell pepper, diced
1/2 red onion, finely chopped
1/2 cup cilantro, chopped
2 limes, juiced
1/4 cup olive oil
1 tsp ground cumin
Salt and pepper to taste
Avocado slices for garnish

Instructions:

In a large bowl, combine cooked quinoa, black beans, red bell pepper, red onion, and cilantro.
In a small bowl, whisk together lime juice, olive oil, ground cumin, salt, and pepper.
Pour the dressing over the quinoa mixture and toss to combine.
Garnish with avocado slices before serving.
Serve chilled or at room temperature. Store in the refrigerator for up to 3 days.

Nutritional Information (per serving):

Calories: Approximately 300 kcal
Protein: 9 g
Fat: 12 g
Carbohydrates: 40 g
Fiber: 8 g
Sugar: 3 g

80. VGN Mediterranean Chickpea Salad

Prep: 15 min | Cook: 0 min | Total: 15 min

Ingredients:

2 cans (15 oz each) chickpeas, drained and rinsed
1 cucumber, diced
1 pint cherry tomatoes, halved
1/2 red onion, thinly sliced
1/2 cup Kalamata olives, pitted and halved
1/2 cup vegan feta cheese, crumbled
1/4 cup parsley, chopped
1/4 cup olive oil
2 lemons, juiced
1 garlic clove, minced
1 tsp dried oregano
Salt and pepper to taste

Instructions:

In a large bowl, combine chickpeas, cucumber, cherry tomatoes, red onion, olives, and parsley.
In a small bowl, whisk together olive oil, lemon juice, minced garlic, oregano, salt, and pepper.
Pour the dressing over the salad and toss to combine.
If using, sprinkle feta cheese over the top.
Serve chilled or at room temperature. Store in the refrigerator for up to 3 days.

Nutritional Information (per serving):

Calories: Approximately 300 kcal
Protein: 10 g
Fat: 15 g
Carbohydrates: 30 g
Fiber: 8 g
Sugar: 5 g

81. VGN Roasted Vegetable and Farro Salad

Prep: 15 min | Cook: 25 min (Roasting & Farro) | Total: 40 min

Ingredients:

2 cups farro, cooked and cooled
2 zucchinis, diced
2 bell peppers, diced
1 red onion, diced
1/4 cup olive oil, divided
2 tbsp balsamic vinegar
1 tsp dried thyme
Salt and pepper to taste
1/4 cup fresh basil, chopped

Instructions:

Preheat the oven to 400°F (200°C). Toss zucchini, bell peppers, and red onion with half of the olive oil, salt, and pepper.

Spread the vegetables on a baking sheet and roast for 20-25 minutes, until tender and caramelized.

In a large bowl, combine cooked farro with roasted vegetables.

Whisk together the remaining olive oil, balsamic vinegar, thyme, salt, and pepper. Pour over the salad and toss to combine.

Garnish with fresh basil.

Serve warm or at room temperature. Store in the refrigerator for up to 3 days.

Nutritional Information (per serving):

Calories: Approximately 300 kcal
Protein: 8 g
Fat: 10 g
Carbohydrates: 45 g
Fiber: 8 g
Sugar: 5 g

82. VGN Avocado and Tomato Salad

Prep: 10 min | Cook: 0 min | Total: 10 min

Ingredients:

3 avocados, diced
2 cups cherry tomatoes, halved
1/4 red onion, thinly sliced
1/4 cup cilantro, chopped
1 lime, juiced
2 tbsp olive oil
Salt and pepper to taste

Instructions:

In a large bowl, gently combine avocados, cherry tomatoes, red onion, and cilantro.

In a small bowl, whisk together lime juice, olive oil, salt, and pepper.

Drizzle the dressing over the salad and toss gently to combine.

Serve immediately or chill in the refrigerator for up to 1 day.

Nutritional Information (per serving):

Calories: Approximately 250 kcal
Protein: 3 g
Fat: 20 g
Carbohydrates: 20 g
Fiber: 8 g
Sugar: 4 g

83. VGN Cucumber and Dill Salad

Prep: 10 min | Cook: 0 min | Total: 10 min + refrigeration

Ingredients:

3 large cucumbers, thinly sliced
1/4 cup fresh dill, chopped
1/4 cup white vinegar
2 tbsp olive oil
1 tbsp sugar
Salt and pepper to taste

Instructions:

In a large bowl, combine the sliced cucumbers and chopped dill.
In a small bowl, whisk together white vinegar, olive oil, sugar, salt, and pepper.
Pour the dressing over the cucumbers and dill, tossing to coat evenly.
Refrigerate for at least 30 minutes before serving to allow the flavors to meld.
Serve chilled. Store in the refrigerator for up to 2 days.

Nutritional Information (per serving):

Calories: Approximately 100 kcal
Protein: 1 g
Fat: 7 g
Carbohydrates: 10 g
Fiber: 2 g
Sugar: 5 g

84. VGN Carrot and Raisin Slaw

Prep: 15 min | Cook: 0 min | Total: 15 min

Ingredients:

6 large carrots, grated
1/2 cup raisins
1/4 cup vegan mayonnaise
2 tbsp lemon juice
1 tbsp sugar
Salt and pepper to taste

Instructions:

In a large bowl, combine grated carrots and raisins.
In a small bowl, mix together vegan mayonnaise, lemon juice, sugar, salt, and pepper.
Pour the dressing over the carrot mixture and toss to combine.
Chill in the refrigerator for at least 1 hour before serving.
Serve cold. Store in the refrigerator for up to 2 days.

Nutritional Information (per serving):

Calories: Approximately 150 kcal
Protein: 1 g
Fat: 7 g
Carbohydrates: 22 g
Fiber: 3 g
Sugar: 15 g

85. VGN Beetroot and Walnut Salad

Prep: 15 min | Cook: 0 min | Total: 15 min

Ingredients:

4 large beetroots, cooked and diced
1 cup walnuts, chopped
1/4 cup balsamic vinegar
2 tbsp olive oil
1 tsp Dijon mustard
Salt and pepper to taste
1/4 cup parsley, chopped

Instructions:

In a large bowl, combine diced beetroots and chopped walnuts.
In a small bowl, whisk together balsamic vinegar, olive oil, Dijon mustard, salt, and pepper.
Pour the dressing over the beetroot and walnut mixture, tossing to coat evenly.
Garnish with chopped parsley.
Serve immediately or chill in the refrigerator for up to 2 days.

Nutritional Information (per serving):

Calories: Approximately 250 kcal
Protein: 6 g
Fat: 20 g
Carbohydrates: 15 g
Fiber: 4 g
Sugar: 9 g

86. VGN Lentil and Roasted Pepper Salad

Prep: 15 min | Cook: 25 min (Lentils) | Total: 40 min

Ingredients:

2 cups lentils, cooked and cooled
1 jar (12 oz) roasted red peppers, drained and sliced
1/4 red onion, thinly sliced
1/4 cup olive oil
3 tbsp red wine vinegar
1 garlic clove, minced
1 tsp dried oregano
Salt and pepper to taste
1/4 cup fresh basil, chopped

Instructions:

In a large bowl, combine cooked lentils, roasted red peppers, and red onion.
In a small bowl, whisk together olive oil, red wine vinegar, minced garlic, oregano, salt, and pepper.
Pour the dressing over the lentil mixture and toss to combine.
Garnish with chopped basil.

Nutritional Information (per serving):

Calories: Approximately 250 kcal
Protein: 12 g
Fat: 10 g
Carbohydrates: 30 g
Fiber: 12 g
Sugar: 4 g

87. VGN Kale and Apple Salad

Prep: 15 min | Cook: 0 min | Total: 15 min

Ingredients:

6 cups kale, stems removed and leaves chopped
2 apples, cored and thinly sliced
1/2 cup dried cranberries
1/2 cup almonds, sliced
For the Dressing:
1/4 cup olive oil
2 tbsp apple cider vinegar
1 tbsp honey or maple syrup
1 tsp Dijon mustard
Salt and pepper to taste

Instructions:

In a large bowl, combine chopped kale, apple slices, dried cranberries, and sliced almonds.
In a small jar, mix together olive oil, apple cider vinegar, honey or maple syrup, Dijon mustard, salt, and pepper. Shake well to combine.
Drizzle the dressing over the salad and toss gently to coat.

Nutritional Information (per serving):

Calories: Approximately 200 kcal
Protein: 4 g
Fat: 12 g
Carbohydrates: 25 g
Fiber: 4 g
Sugar: 15 g

Vegetarian Salad Recipes

88. VGT Caprese Salad with Balsamic Glaze

Prep: 10 min | Cook: 0 min | Total: 10 min

Ingredients:

4 large tomatoes, sliced
1 lb fresh mozzarella cheese, sliced
1/4 cup fresh basil leaves
2 tbsp olive oil
Salt and pepper to taste
1/4 cup balsamic glaze

Instructions:

Arrange tomato and mozzarella slices on a platter, alternating and overlapping them.
Sprinkle fresh basil leaves over the salad.
Drizzle with olive oil and season with salt and pepper.
Drizzle balsamic glaze over the top before serving.
Serve immediately. Best enjoyed fresh.

Nutritional Information (per serving, 6 servings total):

Calories: Approximately 300 kcal
Protein: 18 g
Fat: 20 g
Carbohydrates: 10 g
Fiber: 2 g
Sugar: 6 g

89. VGT Goat Cheese and Beet Salad

Prep: 15 min | Cook: 60 min (Roasting beets) | Total: 1 hr 15 min

Ingredients:

6 medium beets, roasted and sliced
1/2 cup goat cheese, crumbled
1/4 cup walnuts, toasted and chopped
6 cups mixed greens
1/4 cup olive oil
2 tbsp balsamic vinegar
Salt and pepper to taste

Instructions:

Place mixed greens on a serving platter or divide among plates.
Top with sliced beets, crumbled goat cheese, and toasted walnuts.
In a small bowl, whisk together olive oil and balsamic vinegar. Season with salt and pepper.
Drizzle the dressing over the salad.
Serve immediately. Store any leftover ingredients separately in the refrigerator for up to 2 days.

Nutritional Information (per serving):

Calories: Approximately 250 kcal
Protein: 8 g
Fat: 18 g
Carbohydrates: 15 g
Fiber: 4 g
Sugar: 10 g

90. VGT Spinach and Feta Cheese Salad

Prep: 10 min | Cook: 0 min | Total: 10 min

Ingredients:

6 cups fresh spinach leaves
1 cup feta cheese, crumbled
1/2 cup red onion, thinly sliced
1/2 cup walnuts, toasted and chopped
1/4 cup dried cranberries
1/4 cup olive oil
2 tbsp balsamic vinegar
1 tsp honey
Salt and pepper to taste

Instructions:

In a large salad bowl, combine spinach, feta cheese, red onion, walnuts, and dried cranberries.
In a small bowl, whisk together olive oil, balsamic vinegar, honey, salt, and pepper.
Drizzle the dressing over the salad and toss gently.
Serve immediately. Store any leftovers in an airtight container in the refrigerator for up to 1 day.

Nutritional Information (per serving):

Calories: Approximately 250 kcal
Protein: 8 g
Fat: 18 g
Carbohydrates: 15 g
Fiber: 3 g
Sugar: 8 g

91. VGT Caesar Salad with Homemade Croutons

Prep: 15 min | Cook: 10 min (Croutons) | Total: 25 min

Ingredients:

6 cups romaine lettuce, chopped
1 cup homemade croutons (cubed bread, toasted with olive oil and garlic)
1/2 cup Parmesan cheese, grated
1/2 cup Caesar dressing (vegetarian)
Salt and pepper to taste
Lemon wedges for serving

Instructions:

In a large salad bowl, combine romaine lettuce, homemade croutons, and Parmesan cheese.
Add Caesar dressing to the salad and toss until well coated. Season with salt and pepper.
Serve with lemon wedges on the side.
Serve immediately. Store any leftover salad ingredients separately in the refrigerator for up to 1 day.

Nutritional Information (per serving):

Calories: Approximately 300 kcal
Protein: 8 g
Fat: 20 g
Carbohydrates: 20 g
Fiber: 3 g
Sugar: 4 g

92. VGT Broccoli and Cheddar Salad

Prep: 15 min | Cook: 0 min | Total: 15 min

Ingredients:

6 cups broccoli florets
1 cup sharp cheddar cheese, shredded
1/2 cup red onion, finely chopped
1/2 cup raisins
1/2 cup sunflower seeds
1/2 cup mayonnaise
2 tbsp apple cider vinegar
1 tbsp sugar
Salt and pepper to taste

Instructions:

In a large bowl, combine broccoli, cheddar cheese, red onion, raisins, and sunflower seeds.
In a small bowl, whisk together mayonnaise, apple cider vinegar, sugar, salt, and pepper.
Pour the dressing over the broccoli mixture and toss well to coat.
Chill in the refrigerator for at least 30 minutes before serving.
Store in an airtight container in the refrigerator for up to 2 days.

Nutritional Information (per serving):

Calories: Approximately 300 kcal
Protein: 10 g
Fat: 20 g
Carbohydrates: 20 g
Fiber: 3 g
Sugar: 10 g

93. VGT Egg Salad with Dijon Mustard

Prep: 10 min | Cook: 10 min (Eggs) | Total: 20 min

Ingredients:

12 hard-boiled eggs, peeled and chopped
1/2 cup mayonnaise
2 tbsp Dijon mustard
1/4 cup celery, finely chopped
1/4 cup red onion, finely chopped
Salt and pepper to taste
Paprika for garnish
Fresh parsley, chopped, for garnish

Instructions:

In a large bowl, combine chopped eggs, mayonnaise, Dijon mustard, celery, and red onion.
Season with salt and pepper to taste.
Mix well until all ingredients are combined.
Garnish with a sprinkle of paprika and chopped parsley.
Serve chilled. Store in an airtight container in the refrigerator for up to 2 days.

Nutritional Information (per serving):

Calories: Approximately 250 kcal
Protein: 15 g
Fat: 20 g
Carbohydrates: 3 g
Fiber: 0 g
Sugar: 2 g

94. VGT Waldorf Salad

Prep: 15 min | Cook: 0 min | Total: 15 min + refrigeration

Ingredients:

3 medium apples, cored and chopped
1 cup celery, sliced
1/2 cup walnuts, chopped
1/2 cup raisins
1/2 cup mayonnaise
1 tbsp lemon juice
Salt and pepper to taste
Lettuce leaves for serving

Instructions:

In a large bowl, combine apples, celery, walnuts, and raisins.
In a small bowl, mix together mayonnaise and lemon juice. Season with salt and pepper.
Pour the dressing over the apple mixture and toss to coat.
Chill in the refrigerator for at least 30 minutes.
Serve on a bed of lettuce leaves. Store any leftovers in an airtight container in the refrigerator for up to 2 days.

Nutritional Information (per serving):

Calories: Approximately 300 kcal
Protein: 3 g
Fat: 20 g
Carbohydrates: 30 g
Fiber: 4 g
Sugar: 20 g

95.   VGT Greek Salad with Feta

Prep: 15 min | Cook: 0 min | Total: 15 min + refrigeration

Ingredients:

3 large cucumbers, diced
3 tomatoes, diced
1/2 red onion, thinly sliced
1 cup Kalamata olives, pitted
1 cup feta cheese, crumbled
1/4 cup olive oil
2 tbsp red wine vinegar
1 tsp dried oregano
Salt and pepper to taste

Instructions:

In a large salad bowl, combine cucumbers, tomatoes, red onion, and Kalamata olives.
Add crumbled feta cheese to the bowl.
In a small bowl, whisk together olive oil, red wine vinegar, oregano, salt, and pepper.
Pour the dressing over the salad and toss gently.
Chill in the refrigerator for at least 30 minutes before serving.
Store any leftovers in an airtight container in the refrigerator for up to 2 days.

Nutritional Information (per serving):

Calories: Approximately 250 kcal
Protein: 7 g
Fat: 20 g
Carbohydrates: 15 g
Fiber: 3 g
Sugar: 8 g

96.   VGT Arugula and Parmesan Salad

Prep: 10 min | Cook: 0 min | Total: 10 min

Ingredients:

6 cups arugula
1 cup shaved Parmesan cheese
1/4 cup pine nuts, toasted
1/4 cup olive oil
2 tbsp lemon juice
1 tsp honey
Salt and pepper to taste

Instructions:

In a large salad bowl, combine arugula, shaved Parmesan cheese, and toasted pine nuts.
In a small bowl, whisk together olive oil, lemon juice, honey, salt, and pepper.
Drizzle the dressing over the salad and toss gently.
Serve immediately. Store any leftovers in an airtight container in the refrigerator for up to 1 day.

Nutritional Information (per serving):

Calories: Approximately 200 kcal
Protein: 8 g
Fat: 16 g
Carbohydrates: 6 g
Fiber: 2 g
Sugar: 3 g

97. VGT Roasted Butternut Squash Salad

Prep: 15 min | Cook: 30 min (Squash) | Total: 45 min

Ingredients:

4 cups butternut squash, peeled and cubed
6 cups mixed greens
1/2 cup dried cranberries
1/2 cup pecans, toasted
1/4 cup feta cheese, crumbled
1/4 cup olive oil, plus more for roasting
2 tbsp balsamic vinegar
1 tbsp maple syrup
Salt and pepper to taste

Instructions:

Preheat the oven to 400°F (200°C). Toss butternut squash with olive oil, salt, and pepper. Roast for 25-30 minutes until tender.
In a large salad bowl, combine mixed greens, roasted butternut squash, dried cranberries, and toasted pecans.
In a small bowl, whisk together olive oil, balsamic vinegar, and maple syrup.
Drizzle the dressing over the salad and toss gently.
Sprinkle with crumbled feta cheese.
Serve immediately. Store any leftover squash and salad separately in the refrigerator for up to 2 days.

Nutritional Information (per serving):

Calories: Approximately 250 kcal
Protein: 4 g
Fat: 18 g
Carbohydrates: 20 g
Fiber: 4 g
Sugar: 10 g

Meat & Fish Salad Recipes

98. Chicken Caesar Salad

Prep: 15 min | Cook: 20 min (Chicken) | Total: 35 min

Ingredients:

6 boneless, skinless chicken breasts, grilled and sliced
12 cups Romaine lettuce, chopped
1 1/2 cups croutons
3/4 cup Parmesan cheese, grated
Caesar dressing (low-fat), as needed
Salt and pepper to taste

Instructions:

In a large salad bowl, combine the chopped Romaine lettuce, croutons, and Parmesan cheese.
Grill the chicken (about 15/20 min) slice it and place it on the salad.
Drizzle with Caesar dressing and toss to combine.
Season with salt and pepper.
Serve immediately. Store any leftovers in an airtight container in the refrigerator for up to 1 day.

Nutritional Information (per serving):

Calories: Approximately 350 kcal
Protein: 40 g
Fat: 15 g
Carbohydrates: 15 g
Fiber: 3 g
Sugar: 3 g

99. Tuna Niçoise Salad

Prep: 20 min | Cook: 10 min (Eggs & Potatoes) | Total: 30 min

Ingredients:

4 cans (5 oz each) tuna in water, drained and flaked (better if you buy fresh tuna steak)
6 hard-boiled eggs, quartered
2 cups green beans, blanched
3 cups baby potatoes, boiled and halved
1/2 cup Kalamata olives
6 cups mixed greens
For the dressing:

1/4 cup olive oil
3 tbsp red wine vinegar
1 tsp Dijon mustard
1 garlic clove, minced
Salt and pepper to taste

Instructions:

In a large salad bowl, arrange the mixed greens. Top with flaked tuna (if fresh make it seared both sides), hard-boiled eggs, green beans, baby potatoes, and Kalamata olives.
In a small bowl, whisk together olive oil, red wine vinegar, Dijon mustard, minced garlic, salt, and pepper for the dressing.
Drizzle the dressing over the salad just before serving.
Serve immediately. Store any leftovers in an airtight container in the refrigerator for up to 1 day.

Nutritional Information (per serving):

Calories: Approximately 350 kcal, Protein: 30 g, Fat: 15 g, Carbohydrates: 25 g, Fiber: 5 g, Sugar: 5 g

100. Thai Beef Salad

Prep: 20 min | Cook: 10 min (Beef) | Total: 30 min

Ingredients:

1 1/2 lbs flank steak, grilled and thinly sliced
6 cups mixed greens
1 cucumber, sliced
1 red bell pepper, thinly sliced
1/2 cup fresh cilantro, chopped
1/4 cup fresh mint, chopped
For the dressing:
1/4 cup lime juice
2 tbsp fish sauce
1 tbsp soy sauce
2 tsp brown sugar
1 garlic clove, minced
1 red chili, finely chopped

Instructions:

In a large salad bowl, combine mixed greens, cucumber, red bell pepper, cilantro, and mint.
Top with sliced grilled flank steak.
In a small bowl, whisk together lime juice, fish sauce, soy sauce, brown sugar, minced garlic, and chopped red chili for the dressing.
Drizzle the dressing over the salad just before serving.
Serve immediately. Store any leftovers in an airtight container in the refrigerator for up to 1 day.

Nutritional Information (per serving):

Calories: Approximately 300 kcal
Protein: 35 g
Fat: 15 g
Carbohydrates: 10 g
Fiber: 2 g
Sugar: 5 g

101. Grilled Salmon and Avocado Salad

Prep: 15 min | Cook: 10 min (Salmon) | Total: 25 min

Ingredients:

6 salmon fillets (about 4 oz each)
3 avocados, diced
6 cups mixed greens
1/4 cup olive oil, plus extra for grilling
Juice of 2 lemons
Salt and pepper to taste
Fresh dill for garnish

Instructions:

Preheat grill to medium-high heat. Brush salmon fillets with olive oil and season with salt and pepper.
Grill salmon for about 4-5 minutes per side, or until cooked to your liking.
In a large bowl, toss mixed greens with olive oil and lemon juice.
Divide greens onto plates, top with grilled salmon and diced avocado.
Garnish with fresh dill.
Serve immediately. Store any leftovers in the refrigerator for up to 2 days.

Nutritional Information (per serving):

Calories: Approximately 350 kcal
Protein: 25 g
Fat: 25 g
Carbohydrates: 10 g
Fiber: 5 g
Sugar: 2 g

102. Cobb Salad with Chicken

Prep: 20 min | Cook: 20 min (Chicken & Eggs) | Total: 40 min

Ingredients:

3 chicken breasts, cooked and diced
6 cups romaine lettuce, chopped
3 hard-boiled eggs, sliced
1 cup cherry tomatoes, halved
1 avocado, diced
1/2 cup blue cheese, crumbled
6 slices bacon, cooked and crumbled
1/4 cup olive oil
3 tbsp red wine vinegar
1 tsp Dijon mustard
Salt and pepper to taste

Instructions:

Grill the chicken in a pan with some drops of olive oil, boil the eggs.
In a large salad bowl, arrange a bed of romaine lettuce.
Top with rows of diced chicken, sliced eggs, cherry tomatoes, avocado, blue cheese, and crumbled bacon.
In a small bowl, whisk together olive oil, red wine vinegar, Dijon mustard, salt, and pepper.
Drizzle the dressing over the salad just before serving.
Serve immediately. Store any leftovers in an airtight container in the refrigerator for up to 1 day.

Nutritional Information (per serving):

Calories: Approximately 350 kcal
Protein: 30 g
Fat: 22 g
Carbohydrates: 10 g
Fiber: 4 g
Sugar: 3 g

103. Shrimp and Avocado Salad

Prep: 15 min | Cook: 5 min (Shrimp) | Total: 20 min

Ingredients:

1 lb shrimp, peeled and deveined
3 avocados, diced
6 cups mixed greens
1 cup cherry tomatoes, halved
1/4 cup red onion, thinly sliced
1/4 cup cilantro, chopped
2 tbsp olive oil, plus extra for cooking shrimp
Juice of 2 limes
Salt and pepper to taste
Lime wedges for serving

Instructions:

Season shrimp with salt and pepper. In a skillet, heat a tablespoon of olive oil over medium heat and cook shrimp until pink and opaque, about 2-3 minutes per side.
In a large salad bowl, combine mixed greens, cherry tomatoes, red onion, and cilantro.
Add cooked shrimp and diced avocado to the salad.
In a small bowl, whisk together olive oil and lime juice. Season with salt and pepper.
Drizzle the dressing over the salad and toss gently.
Serve with lime wedges. Store any leftovers in the refrigerator for up to 1 day.

Nutritional Information (per serving):

Calories: Approximately 350 kcal
Protein: 25 g
Fat: 22 g
Carbohydrates: 15 g
Fiber: 7 g
Sugar: 4 g

104. Turkey and Cranberry Salad

Prep: 15 min | Cook: 0 min | Total: 15 min

Ingredients:

3 cups cooked turkey, diced
1 cup dried cranberries
6 cups mixed salad greens
1/2 cup walnuts, toasted and chopped
1/4 cup red onion, thinly sliced
1/4 cup olive oil
2 tbsp apple cider vinegar
1 tbsp honey
Salt and pepper to taste

Instructions:

In a large salad bowl, combine mixed greens, diced turkey, dried cranberries, walnuts, and red onion.
In a small bowl, whisk together olive oil, apple cider vinegar, honey, salt, and pepper.
Drizzle the dressing over the salad and toss to combine.
Serve immediately. Store any leftovers in the refrigerator for up to 2 days.

Nutritional Information (per serving):

Calories: Approximately 300 kcal
Protein: 20 g
Fat: 15 g
Carbohydrates: 25 g
Fiber: 4 g
Sugar: 15 g

105. Bacon and Egg Potato Salad

Prep: 20 min | Cook: 20 min (Potatoes & Eggs) | Total: 40 min

Ingredients:

6 large potatoes, boiled and diced
6 hard-boiled eggs, chopped
8 slices bacon, cooked and crumbled
1/2 cup mayonnaise
1/4 cup Dijon mustard
1/4 cup green onions, chopped
Salt and pepper to taste

Instructions:

In a large bowl, combine the diced potatoes, chopped eggs, and crumbled bacon.
In a separate bowl, mix together mayonnaise, Dijon mustard, salt, and pepper.
Pour the dressing over the potato mixture and toss gently to coat.
Sprinkle with chopped green onions.
Serve chilled or at room temperature. Store in an airtight container in the refrigerator for up to 2 days.

Nutritional Information (per serving):

Calories: Approximately 350 kcal
Protein: 12 g
Fat: 20 g
Carbohydrates: 30 g
Fiber: 4 g
Sugar: 2 g

106. Smoked Trout and Arugula Salad

Prep: 15 min | Cook: 0 min | Total: 15 min

Ingredients:

12 oz smoked trout, flaked
6 cups arugula
1/2 red onion, thinly sliced
1/4 cup capers, drained
1/4 cup olive oil
2 tbsp lemon juice
Salt and pepper to taste
Lemon wedges for serving

Instructions:

In a large salad bowl, arrange a bed of arugula.
Top with flaked smoked trout, red onion slices, and capers.
In a small bowl, whisk together olive oil, lemon juice, salt, and pepper.
Drizzle the dressing over the salad just before serving.
Serve with lemon wedges. Store any leftovers in the refrigerator for up to 1 day.

Nutritional Information (per serving):

Calories: Approximately 250 kcal
Protein: 20 g
Fat: 15 g
Carbohydrates: 5 g
Fiber: 2 g
Sugar: 2 g

107. Grilled Chicken and Quinoa Salad

Prep: 20 min | Cook: 30 min (Chicken & Quinoa) | Total: 50 min

Ingredients:

3 cups cooked quinoa, cooled
6 grilled chicken breasts, sliced
6 cups mixed greens
1 cup cherry tomatoes, halved
1 cucumber, diced
1/2 red onion, thinly sliced
1/4 cup fresh parsley, chopped
1/4 cup olive oil
3 tbsp balsamic vinegar
1 tsp honey
Salt and pepper to taste

Instructions:

In a large salad bowl, combine cooked quinoa, mixed greens, cherry tomatoes, cucumber, and red onion.
Top with sliced grilled chicken.
In a small bowl, whisk together olive oil, balsamic vinegar, honey, salt, and pepper.
Drizzle the dressing over the salad and toss gently.
Garnish with chopped parsley.
Serve immediately or store in an airtight container in the refrigerator for up to 2 days.

Nutritional Information (per serving):

Calories: Approximately 350 kcal
Protein: 30 g
Fat: 15 g
Carbohydrates: 25 g
Fiber: 5 g
Sugar: 5 g

Vegan Soup Recipes

108. VGN Classic Vegetable Soup

Prep: 15 min | Cook: 30 min | Total: 45 min

Ingredients:

2 tbsp olive oil, 1 onion, diced, 2 carrots, diced
2 celery stalks, diced, 1 zucchini, diced, 1 bell pepper, diced, 3 garlic cloves, minced
1 cup green beans, trimmed and cut into 1-inch pieces
1 can (14.5 oz) diced tomatoes
6 cups vegetable broth
1 tsp dried basil
1 tsp dried oregano
Salt and pepper to taste
Fresh parsley, chopped for garnish

Instructions:

Heat olive oil in a large pot over medium heat.
Add onion, carrots, celery, zucchini, bell pepper, and garlic. Sauté until vegetables are softened, about 5-7 minutes.
Add green beans, diced tomatoes, vegetable broth, basil, and oregano. Bring to a boil.
Reduce heat to low and simmer for 20-25 minutes, until all vegetables are tender.
Season with salt and pepper.
Garnish with fresh parsley before serving.
Store leftovers in the refrigerator for up to 3 days.

Nutritional Information (per serving):

Calories: 120 kcal, Protein: 3 g, Fat: 4 g, Carbohydrates: 20 g, Fiber: 5 g, Sugar: 6 g

109. VGN Lentil and Tomato Soup

Prep: 10 min | Cook: 40 min | Total: 50 min

Ingredients:

2 tbsp olive oil
1 onion, chopped
2 carrots, diced
2 garlic cloves, minced
1 cup dried lentils, rinsed
1 can (14.5 oz) diced tomatoes
6 cups vegetable broth
2 tsp cumin
1 tsp paprika
Salt and pepper to taste
Fresh cilantro, chopped for garnish

Instructions:

In a large pot, heat olive oil over medium heat. Add onion and carrots, cooking until softened. Stir in minced garlic and cook for another minute.
Add lentils, diced tomatoes, vegetable broth, cumin, and paprika. Bring to a boil.
Reduce heat and simmer for 30-35 minutes, or until lentils are tender.
Season with salt and pepper.
Garnish with chopped cilantro before serving.
Store leftovers in the refrigerator for up to 3 days.

Nutritional Information (per serving):

Calories: 180 kcal
Protein: 9 g, Fat: 4 g
Carbohydrates: 28 g
Fiber: 10 g
Sugar: 6 g

110. VGN Spicy Black Bean Soup

Prep: 10 min | Cook: 25 min | Total: 35 min

Ingredients:

2 tbsp olive oil
1 large onion, diced
2 garlic cloves, minced
2 jalapeños, seeded and minced
3 cans (15 oz each) black beans, drained and rinsed
6 cups vegetable broth
2 tsp ground cumin
1 tsp chili powder
Salt and pepper to taste
Fresh lime juice for serving
Chopped cilantro for garnish

Instructions:

Heat olive oil in a large pot over medium heat. Add onion, garlic, and jalapeños. Cook until softened, about 5 minutes.
Add black beans, vegetable broth, cumin, and chili powder. Bring to a boil.
Reduce heat to low and simmer for 25-30 minutes.
Use an immersion blender to partially blend the soup for a thicker consistency, if desired.
Season with salt and pepper.
Serve with a squeeze of fresh lime juice and garnish with chopped cilantro.
Store leftovers in the refrigerator for up to 3 days.

Nutritional Information (per serving):

Calories: 210 kcal
Protein: 12 g
Fat: 5 g
Carbohydrates: 32 g
Fiber: 12 g
Sugar: 3 g

111. VGN Butternut Squash and Carrot Soup

Prep: 15 min | Cook: 40 min | Total: 55 min

Ingredients:

2 tbsp olive oil
1 butternut squash, peeled and cubed
4 carrots, diced
1 onion, diced
4 cups vegetable broth
1 tsp ground ginger
1/2 tsp nutmeg
Salt and pepper to taste
Coconut cream for serving (optional)

Instructions:

Heat olive oil in a large pot over medium heat. Add butternut squash, carrots, and onion. Cook until slightly softened, about 10 minutes.
Add vegetable broth, ginger, and nutmeg. Bring to a boil.
Reduce heat and simmer until the vegetables are tender, about 20 minutes.
Blend the soup using an immersion blender until smooth.
Season with salt and pepper.
Serve hot, drizzled with coconut cream if desired.
Store leftovers in the refrigerator for up to 3 days.

Nutritional Information (per serving):

Calories: 150 kcal
Protein: 3 g
Fat: 5 g
Carbohydrates: 25 g
Fiber: 6 g
Sugar: 8 g

112. VGN Creamy Broccoli Soup

Prep: 10 min | Cook: 20 min | Total: 30 min

Ingredients:

2 tbsp olive oil
1 onion, chopped
2 garlic cloves, minced
4 cups broccoli florets
3 cups vegetable broth
1 cup almond milk
1/4 cup nutritional yeast (optional, for cheesy flavor)
Salt and pepper to taste
Toasted almond slices for garnish

Instructions:

In a large pot, heat olive oil over medium heat. Add onion and garlic, sautéing until softened.
Add broccoli and vegetable broth. Bring to a boil, then reduce heat and simmer until broccoli is tender, about 10-15 minutes.
Stir in almond milk and nutritional yeast, if using. Simmer for another 5 minutes.
Blend the soup using an immersion blender until smooth.
Season with salt and pepper.
Serve hot, garnished with toasted almond slices.
Store leftovers in the refrigerator for up to 3 days.

Nutritional Information (per serving):

Calories: 130 kcal
Protein: 5 g
Fat: 7 g
Carbohydrates: 14 g
Fiber: 4 g
Sugar: 4 g

113. VGN Mushroom and Barley Soup

Prep: 15 min | Cook: 1 hr | Total: 1 hr 15 min

Ingredients:

2 tbsp olive oil
1 lb mushrooms, sliced
1 onion, diced
2 carrots, diced
2 celery stalks, diced
3/4 cup pearl barley
6 cups vegetable broth
2 tsp thyme leaves
Salt and pepper to taste
Fresh parsley, chopped for garnish

Instructions:

Heat olive oil in a large pot over medium heat.
Add mushrooms, onion, carrots, and celery.
Cook until the vegetables are softened, about 10 minutes.
Add barley, vegetable broth, and thyme. Bring to a boil.
Reduce heat and simmer until the barley is tender, about 30 minutes.
Season with salt and pepper.
Serve hot, garnished with fresh parsley.
Store leftovers in the refrigerator for up to 3 days.

Nutritional Information (per serving):

Calories: 180 kcal
Protein: 6 g
Fat: 5 g
Carbohydrates: 30 g
Fiber: 6 g
Sugar: 4 g

114. VGN Pea and Mint Soup

Prep: 10 min | Cook: 20 min | Total: 30 min

Ingredients:

2 tbsp olive oil
1 onion, chopped
4 cups frozen peas
4 cups vegetable broth
1/4 cup fresh mint leaves, plus extra for garnish
Salt and pepper to taste
Lemon zest for garnish

Instructions:

In a large pot, heat olive oil over medium heat.
Add onion and sauté until softened.
Add frozen peas and vegetable broth. Bring to a boil, then reduce heat and simmer for 10 minutes.
Stir in fresh mint leaves.
Use an immersion blender to puree the soup until smooth.
Season with salt and pepper.
Serve hot, garnished with lemon zest and additional mint leaves.
Store leftovers in the refrigerator for up to 3 days.

Nutritional Information (per serving):

Calories: 150 kcal
Protein: 6 g
Fat: 5 g
Carbohydrates: 20 g
Fiber: 6 g
Sugar: 8 g

115. VGN Sweet Potato and Ginger Soup

Prep: 15 min | Cook: 30 min | Total: 45 min

Ingredients:

2 tbsp olive oil
2 large sweet potatoes, peeled and cubed
1 onion, chopped
2 cloves garlic, minced
1-inch piece ginger, grated
4 cups vegetable broth
1 tsp ground cinnamon
Salt and pepper to taste
Coconut cream for serving (optional)

Instructions:

In a large pot, heat olive oil over medium heat. Add onion, garlic, and ginger, sautéing until fragrant.

Add sweet potatoes, vegetable broth, and cinnamon. Bring to a boil.

Reduce heat and simmer until sweet potatoes are tender, about 20 minutes.

Blend the soup until smooth using an immersion blender.

Season with salt and pepper.

Serve hot, drizzled with coconut cream if desired.

Store leftovers in the refrigerator for up to 3 days.

Nutritional Information (per serving):

Calories: 180 kcal
Protein: 3 g
Fat: 5 g
Carbohydrates: 30 g
Fiber: 5 g
Sugar: 9 g

116. VGN Roasted Red Pepper and Tomato Soup

Prep: 15 min | Cook: 30 min (plus roasting time if applicable) | Total: 45 min

Ingredients:

2 tbsp olive oil
4 red bell peppers, roasted and peeled
2 cans (14.5 oz each) diced tomatoes
1 onion, chopped
2 cloves garlic, minced
4 cups vegetable broth
1 tsp smoked paprika
Salt and pepper to taste
Fresh basil leaves for garnish

Instructions:

In a large pot, heat olive oil over medium heat. Add chopped onion and garlic, sauté until softened.

Add roasted red peppers and canned tomatoes to the pot.

Pour in vegetable broth and add smoked paprika. Stir well.

Bring to a boil, then reduce heat and simmer for 20 minutes.

Use an immersion blender to puree the soup until smooth.

Season with salt and pepper.

Serve hot, garnished with fresh basil leaves.

Store leftovers in the refrigerator for up to 3 days.

Nutritional Information (per serving):

Calories: 120 kcal
Protein: 3 g
Fat: 5 g
Carbohydrates: 18 g
Fiber: 4 g
Sugar: 10 g

117. VGN Coconut Curry Soup

Prep: 15 min | Cook: 30 min | Total: 45 min

Ingredients:

2 tbsp coconut oil
1 onion, chopped
2 cloves garlic, minced
1 tbsp ginger, grated
1 tbsp curry powder
1 can (14.5 oz) coconut milk
4 cups vegetable broth
1 sweet potato, peeled and cubed
1 cup chickpeas, drained and rinsed
2 cups spinach leaves
Salt and pepper to taste
Fresh cilantro for garnish

Instructions:

In a large pot, heat coconut oil over medium heat. Add onion, garlic, and ginger, cooking until fragrant.
Stir in curry powder, cooking for another minute.
Add coconut milk, vegetable broth, sweet potato, and chickpeas. Bring to a boil.
Reduce heat and simmer until sweet potatoes are tender, about 20 minutes.
Stir in spinach leaves until wilted.
Season with salt and pepper.
Serve hot, garnished with fresh cilantro.
Store leftovers in the refrigerator for up to 3 days.

Nutritional Information (per serving):

Calories: 250 kcal
Protein: 6 g
Fat: 15 g
Carbohydrates: 25 g
Fiber: 5 g
Sugar: 7 g

118. VGN Hearty Vegetable and Bean Soup

Prep: 15 min | Cook: 1 hr | Total: 1 hr 15 min

Ingredients:

2 tbsp olive oil
1 onion, diced
2 carrots, diced
2 celery stalks, diced
3 garlic cloves, minced
1 zucchini, diced
1 cup green beans, trimmed and chopped
1 can (15 oz) kidney beans, drained and rinsed
1 can (15 oz) cannellini beans, drained and rinsed
6 cups vegetable broth
1 can (14.5 oz) diced tomatoes
1 tsp dried thyme
1 tsp dried oregano
Salt and pepper to taste
Fresh parsley, chopped for garnish

Instructions:

Heat olive oil in a large pot over medium heat. Add onion, carrots, celery, and garlic. Sauté until softened.
Add zucchini and green beans, cooking for a few more minutes.
Stir in kidney beans, cannellini beans, vegetable broth, diced tomatoes, thyme, and oregano.
Bring to a boil, then reduce heat and simmer for 20-25 minutes.
Season with salt and pepper.
Serve hot, garnished with fresh parsley.
Store leftovers in the refrigerator for up to 3 days.

Nutritional Information (per serving):

Calories: 200 kcal
Protein: 10 g, Fat: 4 g
Carbohydrates: 35 g
Fiber: 10 g, Sugar: 6 g

119. VGN Asian-Inspired Tofu and Vegetable Noodle Soup

Prep: 15 min | Cook: 20 min | Total: 35 min

Ingredients:

2 tbsp sesame oil
1 block firm tofu, cubed
2 cloves garlic, minced
1-inch piece ginger, grated
1 bell pepper, thinly sliced
1 carrot, julienned
4 cups vegetable broth
2 tbsp soy sauce
2 cups bok choy, chopped
4 oz rice noodles
Green onions and sesame seeds for garnish

Instructions:

Heat sesame oil in a large pot over medium heat. Add tofu cubes and cook until golden brown. Remove tofu and set aside.
In the same pot, add garlic and ginger. Sauté until fragrant.
Add bell pepper and carrot, cooking for a few minutes.
Pour in vegetable broth and soy sauce. Bring to a simmer.
Add bok choy and rice noodles. Cook according to noodle package instructions.
Return tofu to the pot and heat through.
Serve hot, garnished with green onions and sesame seeds.
Store leftovers in the refrigerator for up to 2 days.

Nutritional Information (per serving):

Calories: 250 kcal
Protein: 10 g
Fat: 8 g
Carbohydrates: 35 g
Fiber: 3 g
Sugar: 5 g

120. VGN Curried Cauliflower and Chickpea Soup

Prep: 15 min | Cook: 30 min | Total: 45 min

Ingredients:

2 tbsp coconut oil
1 onion, chopped
2 cloves garlic, minced
1 tbsp curry powder
1 head cauliflower, chopped into florets
1 can (15 oz) chickpeas, drained and rinsed
4 cups vegetable broth
1 can (14 oz) coconut milk
Salt and pepper to taste
Fresh cilantro for garnish

Instructions:

In a large pot, heat coconut oil over medium heat. Add onion and garlic, cooking until softened.
Stir in curry powder and cook for an additional minute.
Add cauliflower and chickpeas, stirring to coat with the curry mixture.
Pour in vegetable broth and bring to a boil. Reduce heat and simmer until cauliflower is tender, about 20 minutes.
Add coconut milk and heat through. Blend the soup using an immersion blender until smooth. Season with salt and pepper.
Serve hot, garnished with fresh cilantro.
Store leftovers in the refrigerator for up to 3 days.

Nutritional Information (per serving):

Calories: 250 kcal
Protein: 8 g
Fat: 15 g
Carbohydrates: 25 g
Fiber: 8 g
Sugar: 6 g

121. VGN Spicy Lentil and Kale Soup

Prep: 15 min | Cook: 45 min | Total: 1 hr

Ingredients:

1 cup dried green or brown lentils, rinsed
1 large bunch of kale, stems removed and leaves chopped
1 large carrot, diced
1 onion, chopped
2 cloves garlic, minced
6 cups vegetable broth
2 tablespoons tomato paste
1 teaspoon ground cumin
1 teaspoon chili powder (adjust to spice preference)
1/2 teaspoon smoked paprika
Salt and pepper, to taste
2 tablespoons olive oil
Optional: Lemon wedges for serving

Instructions:

In a large pot, heat olive oil over medium heat. Add onions and carrots, cooking until softened. Add garlic, cumin, chili powder, and smoked paprika. Cook for another minute until fragrant. Stir in the tomato paste, then add the rinsed lentils and vegetable broth. Bring to a boil, then reduce heat and simmer for about 30 minutes. Add the chopped kale to the pot and continue to simmer for another 15 minutes, or until the lentils are tender and the kale is wilted. Season with salt and pepper to taste. Serve hot, with a squeeze of lemon if desired.

Nutritional Information (approximate):

Calories: 250, Fat: 5g, Carbohydrates: 38g
Fiber: 16g, Protein: 15g
Sugar: 3g

Vegetarian Soup Recipes

122. VGT Creamy Potato Leek Soup

Prep: 15 min | Cook: 30 min | Total: 45 min

Ingredients:

2 tbsp olive oil
3 large leeks, cleaned and sliced
5 large potatoes, peeled and diced
6 cups vegetable broth
1 cup heavy cream or almond milk for a vegan alternative
Salt and pepper to taste
Fresh chives for garnish

Instructions:

Heat olive oil in a large pot over medium heat. Add leeks and cook until softened, about 5 minutes.
Add diced potatoes and vegetable broth. Bring to a boil, then reduce heat and simmer until potatoes are tender, about 20 minutes.
Use an immersion blender to puree the soup until smooth.
Stir in heavy cream or almond milk. Season with salt and pepper.
Serve hot, garnished with fresh chives.
Store leftovers in the refrigerator for up to 3 days.

Nutritional Information (per serving):

Calories: 300 kcal, Protein: 6 g, Fat: 12 g
Carbohydrates: 45 g, Fiber: 6 g
Sugar: 5 g

123. VGT French Onion Soup

Prep: 15 min | Cook: 1 hr | Total: 1 hr 15 min

Ingredients:

4 tbsp butter
4 large onions, thinly sliced
6 cups vegetable broth
1/2 cup dry white wine (optional)
1 tsp thyme leaves
6 slices of baguette, toasted
1 cup grated Gruyère cheese (or a vegan alternative)
Salt and pepper to taste

Instructions:

Melt butter in a large pot over medium heat. Add onions and cook, stirring occasionally, until caramelized, about 30 minutes.
Add vegetable broth, white wine (if using), and thyme. Season with salt and pepper. Simmer for 15 minutes.
Preheat the broiler. Ladle the soup into oven-safe bowls.
Top each with a slice of toasted baguette and sprinkle with cheese.
Broil until cheese is melted and bubbly.
Serve hot.
Store any leftovers in the refrigerator for up to 3 days.

Nutritional Information (per serving):

Calories: 350 kcal
Protein: 12 g
Fat: 16 g
Carbohydrates: 40 g
Fiber: 5 g
Sugar: 10 g

124. VGT Tomato Basil Bisque

Prep: 10 min | Cook: 30 min | Total: 40 min

Ingredients:

2 tbsp olive oil
1 onion, chopped
3 cloves garlic, minced
2 cans (14.5 oz each) diced tomatoes
4 cups vegetable broth
1/2 cup fresh basil, chopped
1/2 cup heavy cream or coconut cream
Salt and pepper to taste
Fresh basil leaves for garnish

Instructions:

In a large pot, heat olive oil over medium heat. Add onion and garlic, sauté until softened.
Add diced tomatoes and vegetable broth. Bring to a boil.
Reduce heat and simmer for 15 minutes.
Stir in chopped basil and heavy cream or coconut cream.
Blend the soup using an immersion blender until smooth.
Season with salt and pepper.
Serve hot, garnished with fresh basil leaves.
Store leftovers in the refrigerator for up to 3 days.

Nutritional Information (per serving):

Calories: 180 kcal
Protein: 3 g
Fat: 12 g
Carbohydrates: 15 g
Fiber: 3 g
Sugar: 8 g

125. VGT Cream of Mushroom Soup

Prep: 10 min | Cook: 30 min | Total: 40 min

Ingredients:

2 tbsp butter or olive oil
1 lb mushrooms, sliced
1 onion, chopped
2 cloves garlic, minced
1/4 cup all-purpose flour
4 cups vegetable broth
1 cup heavy cream or almond milk
Salt and pepper to taste
Fresh parsley, chopped for garnish

Instructions:

In a large pot, melt butter or heat olive oil over medium heat. Add mushrooms, onion, and garlic. Cook until mushrooms are browned and onions are translucent.
Stir in flour and cook for 1-2 minutes.
Gradually add vegetable broth, stirring continuously.
Bring to a boil, then reduce heat and simmer for 10 minutes.
Stir in heavy cream or almond milk. Heat through but do not boil.
Season with salt and pepper.
Serve hot, garnished with fresh parsley.
Store leftovers in the refrigerator for up to 3 days.

Nutritional Information (per serving):

Calories: 250 kcal
Protein: 5 g
Fat: 20 g
Carbohydrates: 15 g
Fiber: 2 g
Sugar: 5 g

126. VGT Roasted Butternut Squash Soup

Prep: 20 min | Cook: 45 min | Total: 1 hr 5 min

Ingredients:

1 large butternut squash, peeled, seeded, and cubed
2 tbsp olive oil, divided
1 onion, chopped
3 cloves garlic, minced
4 cups vegetable broth
1 tsp ground cinnamon
1/2 tsp ground nutmeg
Salt and pepper to taste
A dollop of Greek yogurt or coconut cream for serving (optional)

Instructions:

Preheat the oven to 400°F (200°C). Toss butternut squash with 1 tbsp olive oil and spread on a baking sheet. Roast for 25-30 minutes until tender and lightly browned.
In a large pot, heat the remaining olive oil over medium heat. Add onion and garlic, and sauté until softened.
Add the roasted squash, vegetable broth, cinnamon, and nutmeg. Bring to a boil, then reduce heat and simmer for 15 minutes.
Blend the soup using an immersion blender until smooth.
Season with salt and pepper.
Serve hot, topped with a dollop of Greek yogurt or coconut cream, if desired.
Store leftovers in the refrigerator for up to 3 days.

Nutritional Information (per serving):

Calories: 150 kcal
Protein: 3 g, Fat: 5 g
Carbohydrates: 25 g
Fiber: 5 g
Sugar: 8 g

127. VGT Broccoli Cheddar Soup

Prep: 15 min | Cook: 30 min | Total: 45 min

Ingredients:

2 tbsp butter
1 onion, chopped
2 cloves garlic, minced
4 cups broccoli florets
3 cups vegetable broth
1 cup heavy cream or almond milk
2 cups cheddar cheese, shredded
Salt and pepper to taste
Extra cheese for garnish

Instructions:

In a large pot, melt butter over medium heat. Add onion and garlic, sautéing until translucent. Add broccoli and vegetable broth. Bring to a boil, then reduce heat and simmer until broccoli is tender, about 10-15 minutes.

Stir in cream or almond milk and cheddar cheese until the cheese is melted and the soup is heated through.

Blend the soup partially using an immersion blender for a chunky texture.

Season with salt and pepper.

Serve hot, garnished with extra cheese.

Store leftovers in the refrigerator for up to 3 days.

Nutritional Information (per serving):

Calories: 300 kcal
Protein: 15 g
Fat: 25 g
Carbohydrates: 10 g
Fiber: 3 g
Sugar: 5 g

128. VGT Asparagus Cream Soup

Prep: 15 min | Cook: 30 min | Total: 45 min

Ingredients:

2 tbsp butter or olive oil
1 lb asparagus, trimmed and chopped
1 onion, diced
3 cloves garlic, minced
4 cups vegetable broth
1 cup heavy cream or coconut milk
Salt and pepper to taste
Lemon zest and juice for garnish

Instructions:

In a large pot, melt butter or heat olive oil over medium heat. Add asparagus, onion, and garlic. Cook until vegetables are softened, about 10 minutes.

Add vegetable broth and bring to a boil. Reduce heat and simmer for 15 minutes.

Stir in heavy cream or coconut milk, and blend the soup using an immersion blender until smooth.

Season with salt and pepper.

Serve hot, garnished with lemon zest and a squeeze of lemon juice.

Store leftovers in the refrigerator for up to 3 days.

Nutritional Information (per serving):

Calories: 250 kcal
Protein: 5 g
Fat: 20 g
Carbohydrates: 15 g
Fiber: 3 g
Sugar: 6 g

129. VGT Corn Chowder

Prep: 15 min | Cook: 30 min | Total: 45 min

Ingredients:

2 tbsp olive oil
1 onion, chopped
2 potatoes, peeled and diced
4 cups corn kernels (fresh or frozen)
4 cups vegetable broth
1 cup heavy cream or almond milk
Salt and pepper to taste
Fresh chives, chopped for garnish

Instructions:

In a large pot, heat olive oil over medium heat. Add onion and potatoes, cooking until the onion is translucent.
Add corn and vegetable broth. Bring to a boil, then reduce heat and simmer until potatoes are tender, about 15 minutes.
Blend half of the soup using an immersion blender for a creamy texture while leaving the rest chunky.
Stir in heavy cream or almond milk and heat through.
Season with salt and pepper.
Serve hot, garnished with chopped chives.
Store leftovers in the refrigerator for up to 3 days.

Nutritional Information (per serving):

Calories: 300 kcal
Protein: 6 g
Fat: 18 g
Carbohydrates: 30 g
Fiber: 4 g
Sugar: 6 g

130. VGT Beet and Dill Soup

Prep: 20 min | Cook: 1 hr | Total: 1 hr 20 min

Ingredients:

2 tbsp olive oil
1 onion, chopped
3 cloves garlic, minced
4 medium beets, peeled and diced
2 carrots, diced
5 cups vegetable broth
2 tbsp fresh dill, chopped
Salt and pepper to taste
Sour cream or Greek yogurt for serving (optional)

Instructions:

In a large pot, heat olive oil over medium heat. Add onion and garlic, cooking until the onion is translucent.
Add beets and carrots, cooking for a few more minutes.
Pour in vegetable broth and bring to a boil. Reduce heat and simmer until beets are tender, about 20-25 minutes.
Stir in fresh dill and season with salt and pepper.
Blend the soup partially using an immersion blender for a chunky texture.
Serve hot, topped with a dollop of sour cream or Greek yogurt, if desired.
Store leftovers in the refrigerator for up to 3 days.

Nutritional Information (per serving):

Calories: 150 kcal
Protein: 4 g
Fat: 7 g
Carbohydrates: 20 g
Fiber: 5 g
Sugar: 12 g

131. VGT Creamy Zucchini Soup

Prep: 10 min | Cook: 20 min | Total: 30 min

Ingredients:

2 tbsp butter or olive oil
1 onion, chopped
2 cloves garlic, minced
4 medium zucchini, sliced
4 cups vegetable broth
1 cup heavy cream or coconut milk
Salt and pepper to taste
Fresh basil leaves for garnish

Instructions:

In a large pot, melt butter or heat olive oil over medium heat. Add onion and garlic, and sauté until softened.
Add sliced zucchini and cook for 5 minutes.
Pour in vegetable broth and bring to a boil. Reduce heat and simmer until zucchini is tender, about 15 minutes.
Stir in heavy cream or coconut milk.
Blend the soup using an immersion blender until smooth.
Season with salt and pepper.
Serve hot, garnished with fresh basil leaves.
Store leftovers in the refrigerator for up to 3 days.

Nutritional Information (per serving):

Calories: 200 kcal
Protein: 3 g
Fat: 18 g
Carbohydrates: 10 g
Fiber: 2 g
Sugar: 6 g

132. VGT Carrot and Coriander Soup

Prep: 10 min | Cook: 30 min | Total: 40 min

Ingredients:

2 tbsp olive oil
1 onion, chopped
5 large carrots, peeled and chopped
1 potato, peeled and chopped
4 cups vegetable broth
2 tsp ground coriander
Salt and pepper to taste
Fresh coriander (cilantro) for garnish

Instructions:

In a large pot, heat olive oil over medium heat. Add onion and cook until soft.
Add carrots, potato, and ground coriander. Cook for 5 minutes.
Pour in vegetable broth and bring to a boil. Reduce heat and simmer until vegetables are tender, about 20 minutes.
Blend the soup until smooth using an immersion blender.
Season with salt and pepper.
Serve hot, garnished with fresh coriander.
Store leftovers in the refrigerator for up to 3 days.

Nutritional Information (per serving):

Calories: 150 kcal
Protein: 3 g
Fat: 7 g
Carbohydrates: 20 g
Fiber: 5 g
Sugar: 6 g

133. VGT Borscht (Beetroot and Cabbage Soup)

Prep: 20 min | Cook: 1 hr | Total: 1 hr 20 min

Ingredients:

2 tbsp olive oil
1 onion, chopped
2 cloves garlic, minced
3 beets, peeled and grated
2 carrots, grated
1/2 head of cabbage, shredded
6 cups vegetable broth
2 tbsp apple cider vinegar
1 tsp sugar
Salt and pepper to taste
Sour cream or Greek yogurt for serving (optional)
Fresh dill for garnish

Instructions:

In a large pot, heat olive oil over medium heat. Add onion and garlic, sautéing until softened.
Add beets, carrots, and cabbage, cooking for 10 minutes.
Pour in vegetable broth, apple cider vinegar, and sugar. Bring to a boil, then reduce heat and simmer for 30 minutes.
Season with salt and pepper.
Serve hot, with a dollop of sour cream or Greek yogurt and a sprinkle of fresh dill, if desired.
Store leftovers in the refrigerator for up to 3 days.

Nutritional Information (per serving):

Calories: 120 kcal
Protein: 3 g
Fat: 5 g
Carbohydrates: 18 g
Fiber: 4 g
Sugar: 10 g

134. VGT Split Pea Soup

Prep: 10 min | Cook: 1 hr | Total: 1 hr 10 min

Ingredients:

2 tbsp olive oil
1 onion, chopped
2 carrots, diced
2 celery stalks, diced
2 cloves garlic, minced
2 cups dried split peas, rinsed and drained
6 cups vegetable broth
1 bay leaf
1 tsp dried thyme
Salt and pepper to taste
Fresh parsley, chopped for garnish

Instructions:

In a large pot, heat olive oil over medium heat. Add onion, carrots, celery, and garlic, sautéing until softened.
Add split peas, vegetable broth, bay leaf, and thyme. Bring to a boil.
Reduce heat, cover, and simmer until peas are tender, about 1 hour.
Remove bay leaf and blend the soup partially using an immersion blender for a slightly chunky texture.
Season with salt and pepper.
Serve hot, garnished with fresh parsley.
Store leftovers in the refrigerator for up to 3 days.

Nutritional Information (per serving):

Calories: 230 kcal
Protein: 14 g
Fat: 5 g
Carbohydrates: 35 g
Fiber: 15 g
Sugar: 6 g

135. VGT Italian Vegetable and Pasta Soup

Prep: 15 min | Cook: 30 min | Total: 45 min

Ingredients:

2 tbsp olive oil
1 onion, chopped
2 cloves garlic, minced
1 zucchini, diced
1 bell pepper, diced
1 can (14.5 oz) diced tomatoes
4 cups vegetable broth
1 cup small pasta shapes (e.g., macaroni or shells)
1 tsp dried basil
1 tsp dried oregano
Salt and pepper to taste
Grated Parmesan cheese for serving (optional)

Instructions:

In a large pot, heat olive oil over medium heat.
Add onion and garlic, cooking until fragrant.
Add zucchini and bell pepper, cooking for a few more minutes.
Stir in diced tomatoes, vegetable broth, pasta, basil, and oregano.
Bring to a boil, then reduce heat and simmer until pasta is cooked, about 10-15 minutes.
Season with salt and pepper.
Serve hot, topped with grated Parmesan cheese, if desired.
Store leftovers in the refrigerator for up to 3 days.

Nutritional Information (per serving):

Calories: 200 kcal
Protein: 7 g
Fat: 7 g
Carbohydrates: 30 g
Fiber: 4 g
Sugar: 6 g

Meat & Fish Soup Recipes

136. Chicken Noodle Soup

Prep: 15 min | Cook: 30 min | Total: 45 min

Ingredients:

2 tbsp olive oil
1 onion, chopped
2 carrots, diced
2 celery stalks, diced
3 cloves garlic, minced
1 lb chicken breast, diced
6 cups chicken broth
2 cups egg noodles
1 tsp dried thyme
Salt and pepper to taste
Fresh parsley, chopped for garnish

Instructions:

In a large pot, heat olive oil over medium heat.
Add onion, carrots, celery, and garlic, cooking until vegetables are softened.
Add chicken and cook until browned.
Pour in chicken broth and bring to a boil.
Add egg noodles and thyme. Reduce heat and simmer until noodles are tender and chicken is cooked through, about 10-15 minutes.
Season with salt and pepper.
Serve hot, garnished with fresh parsley.
Store leftovers in the refrigerator for up to 3 days.

Nutritional Information (per serving):

Calories: 250 kcal, Protein: 20 g, Fat: 7 g
Carbohydrates: 25 g, Fiber: 3 g, Sugar: 3 g

137. Beef and Barley Soup

Prep: 15 min | Cook: 1 hr | Total: 1 hr 15 min

Ingredients:

2 tbsp olive oil
1 lb lean beef stew meat, cubed
1 onion, chopped
2 carrots, diced
2 celery stalks, diced
3 cloves garlic, minced
6 cups beef broth
3/4 cup pearl barley
1 tsp dried rosemary
Salt and pepper to taste
Fresh parsley, chopped for garnish

Instructions:

In a large pot, heat 1 tbsp olive oil over medium-high heat. Brown the beef cubes, then set aside.
In the same pot, add the remaining olive oil, onion, carrots, celery, and garlic, cooking until softened.
Return beef to the pot. Add beef broth, barley, and rosemary.
Bring to a boil, then reduce heat and simmer until barley and beef are tender, about 45-60 minutes.
Season with salt and pepper.
Serve hot, garnished with fresh parsley.
Store leftovers in the refrigerator for up to 3 days.

Nutritional Information (per serving):

Calories: 300 kcal
Protein: 25 g, Fat: 10 g
Carbohydrates: 25 g
Fiber: 5 g, Sugar: 3 g

138. Clam Chowder

Prep: 20 min | Cook: 30 min | Total: 50 min

Ingredients:

2 tbsp butter
1 onion, chopped
2 celery stalks, diced
3 potatoes, peeled and cubed
4 cups clam juice
2 cans (6.5 oz each) chopped clams, drained with juice reserved
1 cup heavy cream
1/4 cup all-purpose flour
Salt and pepper to taste
Fresh parsley, chopped for garnish

Instructions:

In a large pot, melt butter over medium heat. Add onion and celery, cooking until softened.
Add potatoes and clam juice (including juice reserved from cans). Bring to a boil, then reduce heat and simmer until potatoes are tender, about 15-20 minutes.
In a bowl, whisk together heavy cream and flour. Stir into the soup and cook until thickened.
Add chopped clams and heat through.
Season with salt and pepper.
Serve hot, garnished with fresh parsley.
Store leftovers in the refrigerator for up to 3 days.

Nutritional Information (per serving):

Calories: 350 kcal
Protein: 15 g
Fat: 20 g
Carbohydrates: 30 g
Fiber: 3 g
Sugar: 5 g

139. Italian Sausage and Tortellini Soup

Prep: 15 min | Cook: 30 min | Total: 45 min

Ingredients:

1 lb Italian sausage, casing removed
2 tbsp olive oil
1 onion, chopped
2 garlic cloves, minced
6 cups chicken broth
1 can (14.5 oz) diced tomatoes
9 oz cheese tortellini
2 cups fresh spinach, chopped
Salt and pepper to taste
Grated Parmesan cheese for serving

Instructions:

In a large pot, cook sausage over medium heat until browned. Drain excess fat.
Add olive oil, onion, and garlic to the pot with sausage. Cook until onion is translucent.
Stir in chicken broth and diced tomatoes. Bring to a boil.
Add tortellini and cook according to package instructions.
Stir in spinach and cook until wilted.
Season with salt and pepper.
Serve hot, topped with grated Parmesan cheese.
Store leftovers in the refrigerator for up to 3 days.

Nutritional Information (per serving):

Calories: 300 kcal
Protein: 15 g
Fat: 15 g
Carbohydrates: 25 g
Fiber: 2 g
Sugar: 4 g

140. Chicken and Corn Chowder

Prep: 20 min | Cook: 30 min | Total: 50 min

Ingredients:

2 tbsp butter
1 onion, chopped
2 cloves garlic, minced
2 potatoes, peeled and diced
2 cups corn kernels (fresh, frozen, or canned)
1 lb boneless, skinless chicken breasts, diced
4 cups chicken broth
1 cup heavy cream
Salt and pepper to taste
Fresh chives, chopped for garnish

Instructions:

In a large pot, melt butter over medium heat. Add onion and garlic, cooking until softened.
Add potatoes, corn, and chicken. Cook for 5 minutes, stirring occasionally.
Pour in chicken broth and bring to a boil. Reduce heat and simmer until potatoes are tender and chicken is cooked through, about 20 minutes.
Stir in heavy cream and heat through. Do not boil.
Season with salt and pepper.
Serve hot, garnished with fresh chives.
Store leftovers in the refrigerator for up to 3 days.

Nutritional Information (per serving):

Calories: 300 kcal
Protein: 20 g
Fat: 15 g
Carbohydrates: 25 g
Fiber: 3 g
Sugar: 5 g

141. Shrimp Bisque

Prep: 20 min | Cook: 30 min | Total: 50 min

Ingredients:

2 tbsp olive oil
1 onion, chopped
2 cloves garlic, minced
1 lb shrimp, peeled and deveined
3 tbsp tomato paste
4 cups seafood or vegetable broth
1 cup heavy cream
1/4 cup brandy or sherry (optional)
Salt and cayenne pepper to taste
Fresh parsley, chopped for garnish

Instructions:

In a large pot, heat olive oil over medium heat.
Add onion and garlic, sautéing until translucent.
Add shrimp and cook until pink, about 3-4 minutes. Remove some shrimp for garnish, if desired.
Stir in tomato paste and cook for another minute.
Pour in broth and brandy or sherry if using.
Bring to a boil, then reduce heat and simmer for 15 minutes.
Blend the soup using an immersion blender until smooth.
Stir in heavy cream and heat through without boiling.
Season with salt and cayenne pepper.
Serve hot, garnished with reserved shrimp and fresh parsley.
Store leftovers in the refrigerator for up to 2 days.

Nutritional Information (per serving):

Calories: 350 kcal
Protein: 25 g, Fat: 20 g
Carbohydrates: 15 g
Fiber: 1 g
Sugar: 5 g

142. Turkey and Wild Rice Soup

Prep: 15 min | Cook: 1 hr | Total: 1 hr 15 min

Ingredients:

2 tbsp olive oil
1 onion, chopped
2 carrots, diced
2 celery stalks, diced
3 cloves garlic, minced
1 lb cooked turkey, diced
1 cup wild rice
6 cups turkey or chicken broth
1 tsp dried thyme
Salt and pepper to taste
Fresh parsley, chopped for garnish

Instructions:

In a large pot, heat olive oil over medium heat.
Add onion, carrots, celery, and garlic, cooking until softened.
Add cooked turkey, wild rice, and broth. Stir in thyme.
Bring to a boil, then reduce heat and simmer until the rice is tender, about 45 minutes.
Season with salt and pepper.
Serve hot, garnished with fresh parsley.
Store leftovers in the refrigerator for up to 3 days.

Nutritional Information (per serving):

Calories: 300 kcal
Protein: 25 g
Fat: 10 g
Carbohydrates: 25 g
Fiber: 3 g
Sugar: 3 g

143. Ham and Bean Soup

Prep: 20 min | Cook: 1 hr | Total: 1 hr 20 min

Ingredients:

2 tbsp olive oil
1 onion, chopped
2 cloves garlic, minced
1 cup carrots, diced
1 cup celery, diced
1 lb ham, diced
2 cans (15 oz each) white beans, drained and rinsed
6 cups chicken or vegetable broth
1 tsp dried oregano
Salt and pepper to taste
Fresh thyme, chopped for garnish

Instructions:

In a large pot, heat olive oil over medium heat. Add onion, garlic, carrots, and celery, cooking until vegetables are softened.
Add ham, beans, and broth. Stir in oregano.
Bring to a boil, then reduce heat and simmer for 30 minutes.
Season with salt and pepper.
Serve hot, garnished with fresh thyme.
Store leftovers in the refrigerator for up to 3 days.

Nutritional Information (per serving):

Calories: 350 kcal
Protein: 25 g
Fat: 15 g
Carbohydrates: 30 g
Fiber: 8 g
Sugar: 5 g

144. Thai Coconut Chicken Soup

Prep: 15 min | Cook: 20 min | Total: 35 min

Ingredients:

2 tbsp coconut oil
1 onion, chopped
2 cloves garlic, minced
1-inch piece ginger, grated
1 lemongrass stalk, finely chopped
1 lb chicken breast, thinly sliced
4 cups chicken broth
1 can (14 oz) coconut milk
2 tbsp fish sauce
2 tbsp lime juice
1 tsp sugar
1 red bell pepper, thinly sliced
1 cup mushrooms, sliced
Salt and red chili flakes to taste
Fresh cilantro and lime wedges for garnish

Instructions:

In a large pot, heat coconut oil over medium heat. Add onion, garlic, ginger, and lemongrass, sautéing until fragrant.
Add chicken slices and cook until no longer pink.
Pour in chicken broth and coconut milk. Bring to a simmer.
Stir in fish sauce, lime juice, and sugar. Add red bell pepper and mushrooms. Cook for 5-10 minutes.
Season with salt and red chili flakes.
Serve hot, garnished with fresh cilantro and lime wedges.
Store leftovers in the refrigerator for up to 3 days.

Nutritional Information (per serving):

Calories: 300 kcal, Protein: 25 g, Fat: 18 g, Carbohydrates: 10 g, Fiber: 2 g, Sugar: 5 g

145. Fish Chowder

Prep: 20 min | Cook: 30 min | Total: 50 min

Ingredients:

2 tbsp butter
1 onion, chopped
2 potatoes, peeled and cubed
2 carrots, diced
4 cups fish or vegetable broth
1 lb white fish fillets (e.g., cod or haddock), cubed
1 cup heavy cream or coconut milk
Salt and pepper to taste
Fresh dill or parsley, chopped for garnish

Instructions:

In a large pot, melt butter over medium heat. Add onion, potatoes, and carrots, cooking until vegetables are slightly softened.
Pour in broth and bring to a boil. Reduce heat and simmer until potatoes are tender, about 15 minutes.
Add fish and cook until opaque and flaky, about 5 minutes.
Stir in heavy cream or coconut milk and heat through without boiling.
Season with salt and pepper.
Serve hot, garnished with fresh dill or parsley.
Store leftovers in the refrigerator for up to 2 days.

Nutritional Information (per serving):

Calories: 350 kcal
Protein: 25 g
Fat: 20 g
Carbohydrates: 20 g
Fiber: 3 g
Sugar: 5 g

146. Beef Stew with Root Vegetables

Prep: 20 min | Cook: 2 hrs | Total: 2 hrs 20 min

Ingredients:

2 tbsp olive oil
1 lb beef stew meat, cut into cubes
1 onion, chopped
3 cloves garlic, minced
2 carrots, peeled and diced
2 parsnips, peeled and diced
2 potatoes, peeled and diced
4 cups beef broth
1 tsp dried thyme
1 bay leaf
Salt and pepper to taste
Fresh parsley, chopped for garnish

Instructions:

In a large pot, heat olive oil over medium-high heat. Brown the beef cubes on all sides, then set aside.
In the same pot, add onion and garlic, cooking until softened.
Return beef to the pot. Add carrots, parsnips, potatoes, beef broth, thyme, and bay leaf.
Bring to a boil, then reduce heat and simmer until vegetables are tender and beef is cooked through, about 1-1.5 hours.
Season with salt and pepper.
Serve hot, garnished with fresh parsley.
Store leftovers in the refrigerator for up to 3 days.

Nutritional Information (per serving):

Calories: 350 kcal
Protein: 25 g
Fat: 15 g
Carbohydrates: 30 g
Fiber: 5 g
Sugar: 5 g

147. Spicy Sausage and Lentil Soup

Prep: 15 min | Cook: 1 hr | Total: 1 hr 15 min

Ingredients:

2 tbsp olive oil
1 lb spicy Italian sausage, casing removed
1 onion, chopped
2 carrots, diced
2 celery stalks, diced
3 cloves garlic, minced
1 cup dried lentils, rinsed
4 cups chicken or vegetable broth
1 can (14.5 oz) diced tomatoes
1 tsp smoked paprika
Salt and pepper to taste
Fresh parsley, chopped for garnish

Instructions:

In a large pot, heat olive oil over medium heat. Add sausage and cook, breaking it apart, until browned.
Add onion, carrots, celery, and garlic, cooking until vegetables are softened.
Stir in lentils, broth, diced tomatoes, and smoked paprika.
Bring to a boil, then reduce heat and simmer until lentils are tender, about 30-40 minutes.
Season with salt and pepper.
Serve hot, garnished with fresh parsley.
Store leftovers in the refrigerator for up to 3 days.

Nutritional Information (per serving):

Calories: 300 kcal
Protein: 20 g
Fat: 15 g
Carbohydrates: 25 g
Fiber: 10 g
Sugar: 5 g

148. Chicken Tortilla Soup

Prep: 20 min | Cook: 30 min | Total: 50 min

Ingredients:

2 tbsp olive oil
1 onion, chopped
2 cloves garlic, minced
1 jalapeño, seeded and minced
1 lb chicken breast, diced
4 cups chicken broth
1 can (14.5 oz) diced tomatoes
1 cup corn kernels (fresh or frozen)
1 tsp ground cumin
1 tsp chili powder
Salt and pepper to taste
Tortilla strips, avocado slices, and lime wedges for garnish

Instructions:

In a large pot, heat olive oil over medium heat. Add onion, garlic, and jalapeño, cooking until softened.
Add chicken and cook until no longer pink.
Pour in chicken broth, diced tomatoes, corn, cumin, and chili powder. Bring to a boil.
Reduce heat and simmer for 20-25 minutes.
Season with salt and pepper.
Serve hot, garnished with tortilla strips, avocado slices, and lime wedges.
Store leftovers in the refrigerator for up to 3 days.

Nutritional Information (per serving):

Calories: 250 kcal
Protein: 20 g
Fat: 10 g
Carbohydrates: 20 g
Fiber: 3 g
Sugar: 5 g

149. Pork and White Bean Soup

Prep: 15 min | Cook: 1 hr | Total: 1 hr 15 min

Ingredients:

1 pound lean pork tenderloin, cut into chunks
2 cans (15 oz each) white beans, drained and rinsed
1 onion, chopped
2 carrots, diced
2 celery stalks, diced
4 cups chicken broth
1 can (14.5 oz) diced tomatoes
1 teaspoon smoked paprika
1 teaspoon dried thyme
Salt and pepper, to taste
2 tablespoons olive oil

Instructions:

In a large pot, heat 1 tablespoon of olive oil over medium-high heat. Add pork chunks and brown on all sides. Remove pork and set aside.
In the same pot, add the remaining olive oil, onion, carrots, and celery. Sauté until vegetables are softened.
Add chicken broth, diced tomatoes, smoked paprika, thyme, salt, and pepper. Bring to a boil. Add white beans and browned pork. Reduce heat, cover, and simmer for about 30 minutes, or until the pork is tender.
Adjust seasoning as needed before serving.

Nutritional Information (approximate):

Calories: 300
Protein: 30g
Fat: 8g
Carbohydrates: 29g
Fiber: 6g
Sugar: 4g

Vegan Lunch Recipes

150. VGN Grilled Vegetable and Hummus Wrap

Prep: 15 min | Cook: 10 min | Total: 25 min

Ingredients:

6 whole wheat tortillas
2 zucchinis, sliced lengthwise
2 bell peppers, sliced
1 eggplant, sliced
1 1/2 cups hummus
3 cups baby spinach
2 tbsp olive oil
Salt and pepper to taste

Instructions:

Preheat a grill or grill pan to medium heat. Brush vegetables with olive oil and season with salt and pepper.
Grill vegetables until tender and slightly charred, turning occasionally.
Spread hummus evenly on each tortilla.
Place grilled vegetables and a handful of baby spinach on each tortilla.
Roll up the tortillas tightly, tucking in the edges as you go.
Serve immediately or store in the refrigerator for up to 1 day.

Nutritional Information (per serving):

Calories: Approximately 350 kcal
Protein: 12 g
Fat: 15 g
Carbohydrates: 45 g
Fiber: 10 g
Sugar: 5 g

151. VGN Sushi Rolls

Prep: 30 min | Cook: 20 min (Rice) | Total: 50 min

Ingredients:

6 sheets nori seaweed
3 cups sushi rice, cooked and cooled
1 avocado, sliced
1 cucumber, julienned
1 carrot, julienned
1/2 red bell pepper, julienned
Soy sauce for dipping
Instructions:
Place a nori sheet on a bamboo sushi mat.
Spread a layer of sushi rice over the nori, leaving a small border at the top.
Arrange avocado, cucumber, carrot, and red bell pepper along the bottom of the rice.
Roll the sushi tightly using the bamboo mat.
Slice the roll into 6 pieces and repeat with remaining ingredients.
Serve with soy sauce. Store any leftovers in the refrigerator for up to 1 day.

Nutritional Information (per serving, 1 roll):

Calories: Approximately 300 kcal
Protein: 6 g
Fat: 7 g
Carbohydrates: 55 g
Fiber: 6 g
Sugar: 5 g

152. VGN Mediterranean Falafel Bowl

Prep: 20 min | Cook: 30 min | Total: 50 min

Ingredients:

18 falafel balls (homemade or store-bought)
3 cups quinoa, cooked
1 cucumber, diced
1 pint cherry tomatoes, halved
1 red onion, thinly sliced
3/4 cup hummus
1/2 cup tahini sauce
1/2 cup Kalamata olives, pitted
1/2 cup parsley, chopped
Lemon wedges for serving

Instructions:

Divide the cooked quinoa among 6 bowls.
Top each bowl with 3 falafel balls, diced cucumber, cherry tomatoes, red onion, and a spoonful of hummus.
Drizzle tahini sauce over each bowl.
Garnish with Kalamata olives and chopped parsley.
Serve with lemon wedges. Store any leftovers in separate containers in the refrigerator for up to 2 days.

Nutritional Information (per serving):

Calories: Approximately 350 kcal
Protein: 15 g
Fat: 15 g
Carbohydrates: 45 g
Fiber: 10 g
Sugar: 5 g

153. VGN Spicy Thai Tofu with Rice

Prep: 15 min | Cook: 20 min | Total: 35 min

Ingredients:

2 cups jasmine rice, cooked
1 lb firm tofu, pressed and cubed
2 bell peppers, sliced
1 onion, sliced
2 cloves garlic, minced
2 tbsp soy sauce
2 tbsp Thai red curry paste
1 tbsp ginger, grated
1 can (14 oz) coconut milk
1 tbsp olive oil
Fresh cilantro and lime wedges for garnish

Instructions:

Heat olive oil in a large skillet over medium heat.
Add tofu and cook until golden on all sides.
Add bell peppers, onion, and garlic to the skillet.
Cook until vegetables are tender.
Stir in soy sauce, curry paste, and ginger. Cook for 1 minute.
Pour in coconut milk and bring to a simmer. Cook for 5-7 minutes, or until the sauce thickens slightly.
Serve tofu and vegetables over cooked rice. Garnish with cilantro and lime wedges.
Store leftovers in an airtight container in the refrigerator for up to 2 days.

Nutritional Information (per serving):

Calories: Approximately 350 kcal
Protein: 15 g
Fat: 18 g
Carbohydrates: 35 g
Fiber: 4 g
Sugar: 6 g

154. VGN Burrito with Brown Rice

Prep: 15 min | Cook: 25 min | Total: 40 min

Ingredients:

6 large flour tortillas
3 cups brown rice, cooked
1 can (15 oz) black beans, drained and rinsed
1 cup corn, cooked
1 avocado, sliced
1 cup salsa
1/2 cup vegan cheese, shredded
1/4 cup cilantro, chopped
2 tbsp lime juice
Salt and pepper to taste

Instructions:

Warm the tortillas in a skillet or microwave.
Divide the cooked brown rice among the tortillas.
Top with black beans, corn, avocado slices, salsa, and vegan cheese.
Sprinkle with cilantro and drizzle with lime juice.
Season with salt and pepper.
Roll up the tortillas, folding in the sides as you roll.
Serve immediately or store in the refrigerator for up to 1 day.

Nutritional Information (per serving, 1 burrito):

Calories: Approximately 350 kcal
Protein: 12 g
Fat: 12 g
Carbohydrates: 55 g
Fiber: 10 g
Sugar: 6 g

155. VGN Stuffed Bell Peppers

Prep: 20 min | Cook: 30 min | Total: 50 min

Ingredients:

6 bell peppers, tops removed and seeded
1 cup quinoa, cooked
1 can (15 oz) black beans, drained and rinsed
1 cup corn, cooked
1/2 cup salsa
1 tsp cumin
1 tsp paprika
Salt and pepper to taste
1/4 cup fresh cilantro, chopped

Instructions:

Preheat oven to 375°F (190°C).
In a bowl, mix together quinoa, black beans, corn, salsa, cumin, paprika, salt, and pepper.
Stuff the bell peppers with the quinoa mixture and place them in a baking dish.
Cover with foil and bake for 25-30 minutes, or until peppers are tender.
Garnish with chopped cilantro before serving.
Store any leftovers in the refrigerator for up to 2 days.

Nutritional Information (per serving, 1 stuffed pepper):

Calories: Approximately 250 kcal
Protein: 10 g
Fat: 2 g
Carbohydrates: 45 g
Fiber: 9 g
Sugar: 8 g

156. VGN Pad Thai

Prep: 20 min | Cook: 15 min | Total: 35 min

Ingredients:

12 oz rice noodles, cooked
2 cups bean sprouts
1 cup carrots, julienned
1 red bell pepper, thinly sliced
1/2 cup green onions, chopped
1/4 cup cilantro, chopped
1/4 cup peanuts, crushed
2 tbsp sesame oil
2 cloves garlic, minced
1/4 cup soy sauce
2 tbsp lime juice
2 tbsp brown sugar
1 tbsp peanut butter
1 tsp sriracha (optional)

Instructions:

In a large skillet, heat sesame oil over medium heat. Add garlic, carrots, and bell pepper. Cook until slightly tender.
In a small bowl, whisk together soy sauce, lime juice, brown sugar, peanut butter, and sriracha.
Add the cooked noodles and sauce to the skillet. Toss to combine.
Stir in bean sprouts and green onions. Cook for an additional 2 minutes.
Garnish with cilantro and crushed peanuts before serving.
Serve immediately. Store any leftovers in the refrigerator for up to 2 days.

Nutritional Information (per serving):

Calories: Approximately 350 kcal
Protein: 10 g
Fat: 10 g
Carbohydrates: 55 g
Fiber: 4 g
Sugar: 10 g

157. VGN Chickpea and Avocado Salad Sandwich

Prep: 15 min | Cook: 0 min | Total: 15 min

Ingredients:

1 can (15 oz) chickpeas, drained and mashed
2 avocados, mashed
1/4 cup red onion, finely chopped
1/4 cup cilantro, chopped
Juice of 1 lime
Salt and pepper to taste
12 slices whole grain bread
Lettuce leaves for serving

Instructions:

In a bowl, combine mashed chickpeas, mashed avocados, red onion, cilantro, lime juice, salt, and pepper. Mix well.
Spread the chickpea and avocado mixture on 6 slices of bread.
Top with lettuce leaves and cover with the remaining bread slices to make sandwiches.
Serve immediately or wrap individually for storage in the refrigerator for up to 1 day.

Nutritional Information (per serving, 1 sandwich):

Calories: Approximately 300 kcal
Protein: 10 g
Fat: 12 g
Carbohydrates: 40 g
Fiber: 10 g
Sugar: 5 g

158. VGN Black Bean and Sweet Potato Tacos

Prep: 20 min | Cook: 30 min | Total: 50 min

Ingredients:

6 medium sweet potatoes, peeled and diced
1 can (15 oz) black beans, drained and rinsed
12 corn tortillas
1/4 cup olive oil
1 tsp cumin
1 tsp paprika
Salt and pepper to taste
1/2 cup red onion, finely chopped
1/4 cup cilantro, chopped
Lime wedges for serving

Instructions:

Preheat the oven to 400°F (200°C). Toss sweet potatoes with olive oil, cumin, paprika, salt, and pepper.
Spread sweet potatoes on a baking sheet and roast for 20-25 minutes, or until tender.
Warm the tortillas in a skillet or oven.
Assemble tacos by placing sweet potatoes and black beans on each tortilla.
Top with red onion and cilantro.
Serve with lime wedges. Store any leftover sweet potatoes and black beans in the refrigerator for up to 2 days.

Nutritional Information (per serving, 2 tacos):

Calories: Approximately 350 kcal
Protein: 10 g
Fat: 10 g
Carbohydrates: 55 g
Fiber: 15 g
Sugar: 10 g

159. VGN Moroccan Vegetable Tagine

Prep: 20 min | Cook: 40 min | Total: 1 hr

Ingredients:

1 onion, chopped
2 garlic cloves, minced
2 carrots, sliced
2 zucchini, sliced
1 bell pepper, chopped
1 sweet potato, cubed
1 can (15 oz) chickpeas, drained and rinsed
1 can (14 oz) diced tomatoes
3 cups vegetable broth
1 tsp cumin
1 tsp paprika
1/2 tsp cinnamon
Salt and pepper to taste
1/4 cup raisins
2 tbsp olive oil
Fresh cilantro for garnish

Instructions:

In a large pot or tagine, heat olive oil over medium heat. Add onion and garlic, sauté until softened.

Add carrots, zucchini, bell pepper, sweet potato, chickpeas, diced tomatoes, vegetable broth, cumin, paprika, cinnamon, salt, and pepper. Bring to a boil.

Reduce heat, cover, and simmer for 25-30 minutes, or until vegetables are tender.

Stir in raisins and cook for an additional 5 minutes.

Garnish with fresh cilantro before serving.

Store leftovers in an airtight container in the refrigerator for up to 3 days.

Nutritional Information (per serving):

Calories: Approximately 250 kcal, Protein: 8 g, Fat: 7 g, Carbohydrates: 40 g, Fiber: 10 g, Sugar: 15 g

160. VGN Mushroom Stroganoff

Prep: 15 min | Cook: 20 min | Total: 35 min

Ingredients:

1 lb mushrooms, sliced
1 onion, chopped
2 cloves garlic, minced
2 cups vegetable broth
1 cup coconut milk
3 tbsp soy sauce
1 tbsp paprika
1/2 tsp black pepper
2 tbsp olive oil
2 tbsp cornstarch mixed with 2 tbsp water
Fresh parsley, chopped for garnish
3 cups cooked pasta

Instructions:

In a large skillet, heat olive oil over medium heat. Add onion and garlic, sauté until softened. Add mushrooms and cook until they release their juices and start to brown.

Stir in vegetable broth, coconut milk, soy sauce, paprika, and black pepper. Bring to a simmer.

Add the cornstarch mixture and stir continuously until the sauce thickens.

Serve over cooked pasta and garnish with chopped parsley.

Store any leftover stroganoff in an airtight container in the refrigerator for up to 2 days.

Nutritional Information (per serving):

Calories: Approximately 350 kcal
Protein: 10 g
Fat: 14 g
Carbohydrates: 50 g
Fiber: 4 g
Sugar: 6 g

161. VGN Spiced Lentil and Carrot Burgers

Prep: 20 min | Cook: 10 min | Total: 30 min

Ingredients:

2 cups cooked lentils
1 cup grated carrots
1 onion, finely chopped
2 cloves garlic, minced
1/2 cup breadcrumbs
1 tsp cumin
1 tsp paprika
Salt and pepper to taste
2 tbsp olive oil
6 whole grain burger buns
Lettuce, tomato, and vegan mayo for serving

Instructions:

In a large bowl, mash the lentils slightly. Stir in grated carrots, onion, garlic, breadcrumbs, cumin, paprika, salt, and pepper.
Form the mixture into 6 patties.
Heat olive oil in a skillet over medium heat. Cook the patties for 4-5 minutes per side, or until golden and heated through.
Serve the burgers on whole grain buns with lettuce, tomato, and vegan mayo.
Store any leftover patties in the refrigerator for up to 2 days.

Nutritional Information (per serving, 1 burger with bun):

Calories: Approximately 350 kcal
Protein: 15 g
Fat: 12 g
Carbohydrates: 50 g
Fiber: 10 g
Sugar: 5 g

162. VGN Barbecue Tempeh Sandwiches

Prep: 15 min | Cook: 10 min | Total: 25 min

Ingredients:

1 lb tempeh, sliced
1 cup barbecue sauce
6 whole grain sandwich buns
1/2 cup vegan coleslaw
2 tbsp olive oil
Pickles for serving

Instructions:

Heat olive oil in a skillet over medium heat. Add tempeh slices and cook until golden on both sides.
Brush barbecue sauce over the tempeh and continue to cook for another 2-3 minutes. Toast the sandwich buns. Assemble sandwiches by placing barbecue tempeh on buns, topped with vegan coleslaw and pickles.
Serve immediately. Store any leftover tempeh in the refrigerator for up to 2 days.

Nutritional Information (per serving, 1 sandwich):

Calories: Approximately 350 kcal
Protein: 20 g
Fat: 12 g
Carbohydrates: 45 g
Fiber: 5 g
Sugar: 15 g

163. VGN Buddha Bowl

Prep: 20 min | Cook: 30 min | Total: 50 min

Ingredients:

3 cups quinoa, cooked
1 can (15 oz) chickpeas, drained and rinsed
1 avocado, sliced
2 cups spinach, raw
1 cup cherry tomatoes, halved
1 cucumber, sliced
1/4 cup tahini
Juice of 1 lemon
2 tbsp maple syrup
Salt and pepper to taste
1/4 cup pumpkin seeds

Instructions:

Divide the cooked quinoa among 6 bowls.
Top each bowl with chickpeas, avocado slices, spinach, cherry tomatoes, and cucumber slices.
In a small bowl, whisk together tahini, lemon juice, maple syrup, salt, and pepper to make a dressing.
Drizzle the dressing over each bowl.
Sprinkle pumpkin seeds on top.
Serve immediately. Store any leftovers in separate containers in the refrigerator for up to 2 days.

Nutritional Information (per serving):

Calories: Approximately 350 kcal
Protein: 15 g
Fat: 15 g
Carbohydrates: 45 g
Fiber: 10 g
Sugar: 10 g

164. VGN Korean Bibimbap with Tofu

Prep: 30 min | Cook: 20 min | Total: 50 min

Ingredients:

3 cups brown rice, cooked
1 lb firm tofu, pressed and cubed
2 cups spinach, blanched
1 carrot, julienned
1 cucumber, sliced
1 zucchini, sliced
1/4 cup soy sauce
2 tbsp sesame oil
2 tbsp gochujang (Korean chili paste)
1 tbsp rice vinegar
1 tbsp sugar
2 cloves garlic, minced
1 tbsp sesame seeds
6 fried vegan eggs (made from tofu or vegan egg substitute), optional

Instructions:

In a skillet, heat 1 tablespoon sesame oil over medium heat. Cook tofu until golden on all sides.
In a small bowl, mix soy sauce, 1 tablespoon sesame oil, gochujang, rice vinegar, sugar, and garlic to make a sauce.
Divide the cooked rice among 6 bowls.
Top each bowl with tofu, spinach, carrot, cucumber, and zucchini.
Drizzle the sauce over each bowl and sprinkle with sesame seeds.
Optionally, top each bowl with a fried vegan egg.
Serve immediately. Store any leftovers in separate containers in the refrigerator for up to 2 days.

Nutritional Information (per serving):

Calories: Approximately 350 kcal, Protein: 15 g
Fat: 12 g, Carbohydrates: 50 g, Fiber: 8 g, Sugar: 10 g

Vegetarian Lunch Recipes

165. VGT Spinach and Ricotta Stuffed Pasta Shells

Prep: 30 min | Cook: 30 min | Total: 1 hr

Ingredients:

24 jumbo pasta shells, 2 cups ricotta cheese
2 cups spinach, cooked and chopped, 1 cup mozzarella cheese, shredded, 1/2 cup Parmesan cheese, grated, 2 cups marinara sauce, 1 egg, 2 cloves garlic, minced, Salt and pepper to taste, Fresh basil for garnish

Instructions:

Preheat the oven to 375°F (190°C). Cook pasta shells according to package instructions until al dente.
In a bowl, mix ricotta, spinach, half of the mozzarella, Parmesan, egg, garlic, salt, and pepper.
Spread a thin layer of marinara sauce in the bottom of a baking dish.
Stuff each pasta shell with the ricotta mixture and place in the baking dish.
Pour the remaining marinara sauce over the shells and sprinkle with the remaining mozzarella.
Bake for 25-30 minutes, or until bubbly and golden.
Garnish with fresh basil before serving.
Store leftovers in an airtight container in the refrigerator for up to 2 days.

Nutritional Information (per serving):

Calories: Approximately 350 kcal, Protein: 18 g, Fat: 15 g, Carbohydrates: 35 g, Fiber: 3 g, Sugar: 5 g

166. VGT Lasagna

Prep: 30 min | Cook: 45 min | Total: 1 hr 15 min

Ingredients:

12 lasagna noodles
2 cups ricotta cheese
2 cups spinach, cooked and chopped
1 zucchini, sliced
1 bell pepper, chopped
3 cups marinara sauce
2 cups mozzarella cheese, shredded
1/2 cup Parmesan cheese, grated
1 egg
Salt and pepper to taste

Instructions:

Preheat the oven to 375°F (190°C). Cook lasagna noodles according to package instructions until al dente.
In a bowl, mix ricotta, spinach, egg, salt, and pepper.
Spread a layer of marinara sauce in the bottom of a baking dish.
Layer noodles, ricotta mixture, zucchini, bell pepper, and marinara sauce. Repeat layers.
Top with mozzarella and Parmesan cheeses.
Cover with foil and bake for 30 minutes.
Remove foil and bake for another 15 minutes.
Let cool before serving. Store leftovers in the refrigerator for up to 2 days.

Nutritional Information (per serving):

Calories: Approximately 350 kcal
Protein: 20 g
Fat: 15 g
Carbs: 40 g
Fiber: 4 g
Sugar: 6 g

167. VGT Goat Cheese and Spinach Quiche

Prep: 20 min | Cook: 40 min | Total: 1 hr

Ingredients:

1 pre-made pie crust
4 large eggs
1 cup heavy cream
2 cups spinach, cooked and drained
1 cup goat cheese, crumbled
1/2 cup cherry tomatoes, halved
Salt and pepper to taste
Nutmeg, a pinch

Instructions:

Preheat the oven to 375°F (190°C).
Place the pie crust in a 9-inch pie dish.
In a bowl, whisk together eggs, heavy cream, salt, pepper, and nutmeg.
Stir in spinach and half of the goat cheese.
Pour the egg mixture into the pie crust. Top with cherry tomatoes and the remaining goat cheese.
Bake for 35-40 minutes, or until the quiche is set and the crust is golden.
Let cool before serving.
Store leftovers in the refrigerator for up to 2 days.

Nutritional Information (per serving):

Calories: Approximately 350 kcal
Protein: 15 g
Fat: 25 g
Carbohydrates: 15 g
Fiber: 1 g
Sugar: 3 g

168. VGT Greek Spanakopita

Prep: 30 min | Cook: 30 min | Total: 1 hr

Ingredients:

1 package phyllo dough, thawed
2 cups spinach, cooked and squeezed dry
1 cup feta cheese, crumbled
1/2 cup onions, finely chopped
2 eggs, beaten
1/4 cup olive oil
1/4 cup fresh dill, chopped
Salt and pepper to taste
Melted butter for brushing

Instructions:

Preheat the oven to 375°F (190°C).
In a bowl, mix spinach, feta cheese, onions, eggs, olive oil, dill, salt, and pepper.
Lay a sheet of phyllo dough on a flat surface and brush with melted butter. Place a spoonful of the spinach mixture on one end and fold into a triangle.
Place the triangles on a baking sheet.
Bake for 20-25 minutes, or until golden and crispy.
Serve warm. Store any leftovers in the refrigerator for up to 2 days.

Nutritional Information (per serving, 2 triangles):

Calories: Approximately 300 kcal
Protein: 8 g
Fat: 18 g
Carbohydrates: 25 g
Fiber: 2 g
Sugar: 2 g

169. VGT Caprese Panini

Prep: 5 min | Cook: 10 min | Total: 15 min

Ingredients:

12 slices whole grain bread
2 large tomatoes, sliced
1 ball fresh mozzarella cheese, sliced
1/4 cup fresh basil leaves
Balsamic glaze
Salt and pepper to taste
Olive oil for brushing

Instructions:

Preheat a panini press or grill pan.
Assemble sandwiches with bread, tomato slices, mozzarella, and basil leaves. Drizzle with balsamic glaze and season with salt and pepper.
Brush the outside of the bread with olive oil.
Grill each panini until the bread is toasted and the cheese is melted.
Serve immediately. Store any leftover ingredients separately in the refrigerator.

Nutritional Information (per serving, 1 sandwich):

Calories: Approximately 300 kcal
Protein: 15 g
Fat: 15 g
Carbohydrates: 30 g
Fiber: 5 g
Sugar: 5 g

170. VGT Mushroom Risotto

Prep: 10 min | Cook: 30 min | Total: 40 min

Ingredients:

1 1/2 cups Arborio rice
4 cups vegetable broth, warmed
2 cups mushrooms, sliced
1 onion, finely chopped
2 cloves garlic, minced
1/2 cup white wine
1/2 cup Parmesan cheese, grated
2 tbsp olive oil
Salt and pepper to taste
Fresh parsley, chopped for garnish

Instructions:

In a large pan, heat olive oil over medium heat.
Add onions and garlic, sauté until soft.
Add mushrooms and cook until tender.
Stir in Arborio rice and cook for 1-2 minutes.
Add white wine and stir until absorbed.
Gradually add warm vegetable broth, one ladle at a time, stirring constantly until each ladle is absorbed before adding the next.
Once all the broth is absorbed and the rice is creamy, stir in Parmesan cheese. Season with salt and pepper.
Garnish with fresh parsley before serving.
Store leftovers in an airtight container in the refrigerator for up to 2 days.

Nutritional Information (per serving):

Calories: Approximately 350 kcal
Protein: 10 g
Fat: 12 g
Carbohydrates: 50 g
Fiber: 3 g
Sugar: 3 g

171. VGT Cauliflower and Cheese Bake

Prep: 15 min | Cook: 30 min | Total: 45 min

Ingredients:

1 large head cauliflower, cut into florets
2 cups cheddar cheese, shredded
1 cup milk
1/2 cup heavy cream
1/4 cup breadcrumbs
2 tbsp butter
2 cloves garlic, minced
1 tsp mustard powder
Salt and pepper to taste
Fresh parsley, chopped for garnish

Instructions:

Preheat the oven to 375°F (190°C).
Steam cauliflower florets until just tender, about 5-7 minutes.
In a saucepan, melt butter over medium heat. Add garlic and cook for 1 minute.
Stir in milk, heavy cream, and mustard powder. Bring to a simmer.
Gradually add 1 1/2 cups of cheese, stirring until melted and smooth.
Season with salt and pepper.
Place cauliflower in a baking dish. Pour cheese sauce over the top.
Sprinkle with breadcrumbs and the remaining cheese.
Bake for 20-25 minutes, until golden and bubbly.
Garnish with fresh parsley before serving.
Store leftovers in the refrigerator for up to 2 days.

Nutritional Information (per serving):

Calories: Approximately 350 kcal, Protein: 15 g, Fat: 25 g, Carbohydrates: 20 g, Fiber: 4 g, Sugar: 6 g

172. VGT Taco Salad

Prep: 15 min | Cook: 10 min | Total: 25 min

Ingredients:

6 cups romaine lettuce, chopped
1 can (15 oz) black beans, drained and rinsed
1 cup corn, cooked
1 cup cherry tomatoes, halved
1 avocado, diced
1/2 cup cheddar cheese, shredded
1/2 cup salsa
1/4 cup sour cream
1/4 cup cilantro, chopped
1 lime, juiced
Tortilla chips for serving
Salt and pepper to taste

Instructions:

In a large salad bowl, combine romaine lettuce, black beans, corn, cherry tomatoes, and avocado.
Top with shredded cheese and a dollop of sour cream.
Drizzle with salsa and lime juice.
Sprinkle with cilantro.
Serve with tortilla chips on the side.
Toss gently before serving.
Store any leftovers in the refrigerator for up to 1 day.

Nutritional Information (per serving):

Calories: Approximately 300 kcal
Protein: 12 g
Fat: 15 g
Carbohydrates: 35 g
Fiber: 10 g
Sugar: 5 g

173. VGT Eggplant Parmesan

Prep: 20 min | Cook: 30 min | Total: 50 min

Ingredients:

2 large eggplants, sliced into 1/2 inch rounds
3 cups marinara sauce
2 cups mozzarella cheese, shredded
1 cup Parmesan cheese, grated
1 cup all-purpose flour
2 large eggs, beaten
2 cups breadcrumbs
Salt and pepper to taste
Olive oil for frying
Fresh basil for garnish

Instructions:

Season eggplant slices with salt and let sit for 20 minutes to draw out moisture. Pat dry.
Dredge eggplant slices in flour, dip in beaten eggs, and coat with breadcrumbs.
Heat olive oil in a skillet and fry eggplant slices until golden on both sides. Drain on paper towels.
Preheat the oven to 375°F (190°C).
Spread a layer of marinara sauce in a baking dish. Layer fried eggplant, more sauce, mozzarella, and Parmesan. Repeat layers.
Bake for 30 minutes, or until bubbly and golden.
Garnish with fresh basil before serving.
Store leftovers in the refrigerator for up to 2 days.

Nutritional Information (per serving):

Calories: Approximately 350 kcal
Protein: 18 g
Fat: 18 g
Carbohydrates: 30 g
Fiber: 5 g
Sugar: 8 g

174. VGT Cheese and Vegetable Quesadilla

Prep: 10 min | Cook: 10 min | Total: 20 min

Ingredients:

12 large flour tortillas
2 cups cheddar cheese, shredded
1 bell pepper, sliced
1 onion, sliced
1 zucchini, sliced
1 cup mushrooms, sliced
1/2 cup salsa
2 tbsp olive oil
Salt and pepper to taste
Sour cream for serving

Instructions:

In a skillet, heat 1 tablespoon olive oil. Sauté bell pepper, onion, zucchini, and mushrooms until tender. Season with salt and pepper.
On a tortilla, spread a layer of cheese, cooked vegetables, and a spoonful of salsa. Top with another tortilla.
In a clean skillet, cook the quesadilla until golden on each side and the cheese is melted.
Cut into wedges and serve with sour cream.
Store any leftover filling in the refrigerator for up to 2 days.

Nutritional Information (per serving, 1 quesadilla):

Calories: Approximately 350 kcal
Protein: 15 g
Fat: 18 g
Carbohydrates: 35 g
Fiber: 3 g
Sugar: 5 g

175. VGT Spinach and Feta Quiche with Sweet Potato Crust

Prep: 20 min | Cook: 45 min | Total: 1 hr 5 min

Ingredients:

2 large sweet potatoes, peeled and thinly sliced
4 eggs
1 cup heavy cream or almond milk
2 cups fresh spinach, chopped
1 cup feta cheese, crumbled
1/4 cup red onion, finely chopped
Salt and pepper to taste
Olive oil for greasing

Instructions:

Preheat the oven to 375°F (190°C). Grease a pie dish with olive oil.
Layer the sweet potato slices at the bottom and sides of the dish to form a crust.
Bake the sweet potato crust for 20 minutes.
In a bowl, whisk together eggs, cream or almond milk, spinach, feta cheese, and red onion. Season with salt and pepper.
Pour the egg mixture into the sweet potato crust.
Bake for 35-40 minutes until the quiche is set and golden.
Serve warm or store in the refrigerator for up to 3 days.

Nutritional Information (per serving):

Calories: 300 kcal
Protein: 12 g
Fat: 20 g
Carbohydrates: 20 g
Fiber: 3 g
Sugar: 6 g

176. VGT Baked Macaroni and Cheese

Prep: 15 min | Cook: 30 min | Total: 45 min

Ingredients:

1 lb macaroni pasta
4 cups cheddar cheese, shredded
2 cups milk
1/4 cup butter
1/4 cup all-purpose flour
1/2 tsp mustard powder
Salt and pepper to taste
1/2 cup breadcrumbs
1/4 cup Parmesan cheese, grated

Instructions:

Preheat the oven to 375°F (190°C). Cook macaroni according to package instructions until al dente.
In a saucepan, melt butter over medium heat. Add flour and mustard powder, stirring to form a roux.
Gradually add milk, whisking continuously until the sauce thickens.
Stir in 3 cups of cheddar cheese until melted. Season with salt and pepper.
Combine cooked macaroni with cheese sauce and transfer to a baking dish.
Top with remaining cheddar cheese, breadcrumbs, and Parmesan cheese.
Bake for 25-30 minutes, or until golden and bubbly.
Serve hot. Store leftovers in the refrigerator for up to 2 days.

Nutritional Information (per serving):

Calories: Approximately 350 kcal
Protein: 18 g
Fat: 18 g
Carbohydrates: 35 g
Fiber: 2 g
Sugar: 5 g

177. VGT Stuffed Zucchini Boats

Prep: 20 min | Cook: 25 min | Total: 45 min

Ingredients:

6 medium zucchini, halved lengthwise
1 cup ricotta cheese
1 cup spinach, cooked and chopped
1/2 cup Parmesan cheese, grated
1 cup marinara sauce
1/2 cup mozzarella cheese, shredded
2 cloves garlic, minced
Salt and pepper to taste
Olive oil for brushing

Instructions:

Preheat the oven to 375°F (190°C). Scoop out the insides of the zucchini halves to create boats.
In a bowl, mix together ricotta, spinach, Parmesan, garlic, salt, and pepper.
Fill each zucchini boat with the ricotta mixture.
Place the stuffed zucchini in a baking dish and spoon marinara sauce over each.
Sprinkle with mozzarella cheese.
Brush the outside of the zucchini with olive oil.
Bake for 20-25 minutes, or until zucchini is tender and cheese is melted and bubbly.
Serve warm. Store leftovers in the refrigerator for up to 2 days.

Nutritional Information (per serving, 1 zucchini boat):

Calories: Approximately 250 kcal
Protein: 12 g
Fat: 15 g
Carbohydrates: 20 g
Fiber: 3 g
Sugar: 5 g

178. VGT Thai Green Curry

Prep: 15 min | Cook: 20 min | Total: 35 min

Ingredients:

2 cans (14 oz each) coconut milk
1/4 cup Thai green curry paste
2 cups broccoli florets
1 bell pepper, sliced
1 carrot, sliced
1 cup snap peas
1 block firm tofu, pressed and cubed
2 tbsp soy sauce
1 tbsp sugar
1 lime, juiced
1/4 cup basil leaves, chopped
3 cups cooked jasmine rice

Instructions:

In a large pot, heat a tablespoon of coconut milk over medium heat. Stir in green curry paste and cook for 1 minute.
Add the remaining coconut milk, broccoli, bell pepper, carrot, snap peas, tofu, soy sauce, and sugar. Bring to a simmer.
Cook for 10-15 minutes, or until vegetables are tender.
Stir in lime juice and basil leaves.
Serve over jasmine rice. Store any leftovers in the refrigerator for up to 2 days.

Nutritional Information (per serving):

Calories: Approximately 350 kcal
Protein: 12 g
Fat: 18 g
Carbohydrates: 35 g
Fiber: 4 g
Sugar: 6 g

179. VGT Broccoli and Cheese Tart

Prep: 20 min | Cook: 30 min | Total: 50 min

Ingredients:

1 pre-made pie crust
2 cups broccoli florets, steamed
1 cup cheddar cheese, shredded
1/2 cup heavy cream
3 eggs
1/2 tsp nutmeg
Salt and pepper to taste
1/4 cup Parmesan cheese, grated

Instructions:

Preheat the oven to 375°F (190°C).
Place the pie crust in a 9-inch tart pan.
In a bowl, beat together eggs, heavy cream, nutmeg, salt, and pepper.
Layer steamed broccoli and cheddar cheese in the pie crust.
Pour the egg mixture over the broccoli and cheese.
Sprinkle with Parmesan cheese.
Bake for 30-35 minutes, or until the filling is set and the crust is golden.
Let cool before serving.
Store leftovers in the refrigerator for up to 2 days.

Nutritional Information (per serving, 1 slice):

Calories: Approximately 300 kcal
Protein: 12 g
Fat: 20 g
Carbohydrates: 20 g
Fiber: 2 g
Sugar: 2 g

Meat & Fish Lunch Recipes

180. Grilled Chicken Caesar Salad Wrap

Prep: 15 min | Cook: 10 min | Total: 25 min

Ingredients:

3 chicken breasts, grilled and sliced
6 large whole wheat tortillas
6 cups romaine lettuce, chopped
1/2 cup Caesar dressing, light
1/2 cup Parmesan cheese, grated
Croutons for crunch (optional)
Salt and pepper to taste

Instructions:

Toss the chopped romaine lettuce with Caesar dressing, Parmesan cheese, salt, and pepper.
Lay out the tortillas and divide the salad among them.
Top with slices of grilled chicken and croutons, if desired.
Roll up the tortillas tightly, folding in the sides as you roll.
Cut each wrap in half and serve.
Store any leftovers in the refrigerator for up to 2 days.

Nutritional Information (per serving, 1 wrap):

Calories: Approximately 350 kcal
Protein: 25 g
Fat: 15 g
Carbohydrates: 30 g
Fiber: 5 g
Sugar: 3 g

181. Turkey Burgers with Sweet Potato

Prep: 20 min | Cook: 30 min | Total: 50 min

Ingredients:

1.5 lbs ground turkey
6 whole wheat burger buns
1 tbsp Worcestershire sauce
1 tsp garlic powder
1 tsp onion powder
Salt and pepper to taste
3 large sweet potatoes, cut into fries
2 tbsp olive oil

Instructions:

Preheat the oven to 425°F (220°C). Toss sweet potato fries with olive oil, salt, and pepper. Spread on a baking sheet and bake for 20-25 minutes, flipping halfway through.
In a bowl, mix ground turkey with Worcestershire sauce, garlic powder, onion powder, salt, and pepper.
Form into 6 patties and grill or cook in a skillet until fully cooked.
Serve burgers on whole wheat buns with sweet potato fries.
Store any leftovers in the refrigerator for up to 3 days.

Nutritional Information (per serving, 1 burger with fries):

Calories: Approximately 350 kcal
Protein: 30 g
Fat: 12 g
Carbohydrates: 35 g
Fiber: 5 g
Sugar: 8 g

182. Tuna and White Bean Salad

Prep: 15 min | Cook: 0 min | Total: 15 min

Ingredients:

2 cans (5 oz each) tuna in water, drained
1 can (15 oz) white beans, drained and rinsed
1 red bell pepper, diced
1/2 red onion, finely chopped
1/4 cup parsley, chopped
1/4 cup olive oil
Juice of 1 lemon
Salt and pepper to taste

Instructions:

In a large bowl, combine tuna, white beans, red bell pepper, red onion, and parsley.
In a small bowl, whisk together olive oil and lemon juice. Season with salt and pepper.
Pour the dressing over the tuna mixture and toss to combine.
Serve chilled or at room temperature.
Store in the refrigerator for up to 3 days.

Nutritional Information (per serving):

Calories: Approximately 350 kcal
Protein: 25 g
Fat: 15 g
Carbohydrates: 30 g
Fiber: 8 g
Sugar: 3 g

183. Beef Stir-Fry with Broccoli

Prep: 15 min | Cook: 15 min | Total: 30 min

Ingredients:

1 lb beef sirloin, thinly sliced
4 cups broccoli florets
1 red bell pepper, sliced
1 onion, sliced
2 cloves garlic, minced
1/4 cup soy sauce
2 tbsp oyster sauce
1 tbsp sesame oil
1 tbsp ginger, grated
2 tsp cornstarch
2 tbsp water
3 cups cooked brown rice

Instructions:

In a bowl, mix soy sauce, oyster sauce, sesame oil, ginger, cornstarch, and water.
Heat a wok or large skillet over high heat. Add beef and stir-fry until browned. Remove from the wok.
Add broccoli, bell pepper, onion, and garlic to the wok. Stir-fry until vegetables are tender-crisp.
Return the beef to the wok. Add the sauce and stir until thickened.
Serve over cooked brown rice.

Nutritional Information (per serving):

Calories: Approximately 350 kcal
Protein: 30 g
Fat: 15 g
Carbohydrates: 30 g
Fiber: 4 g
Sugar: 5 g

184. Chicken Tacos with Avocado

Prep: 20 min | Cook: 10 min | Total: 30 min

Ingredients:

12 small corn tortillas
1 lb chicken breasts, cooked and shredded
2 avocados, diced
1 cup cabbage, shredded
1/2 cup salsa
1/4 cup cilantro, chopped
2 limes, cut into wedges
Salt and pepper to taste

Instructions:

Warm the tortillas in a skillet or oven.
Assemble the tacos by placing shredded chicken, diced avocado, and shredded cabbage on each tortilla.
Top with salsa and cilantro.
Squeeze lime juice over the tacos and season with salt and pepper.
Serve with lime wedges.

Nutritional Information (per serving, 2 tacos):

Calories: Approximately 300 kcal
Protein: 20 g
Fat: 12 g
Carbohydrates: 30 g
Fiber: 6 g
Sugar: 2 g

185. Shrimp and Avocado Rice Bowl

Prep: 20 min | Cook: 10 min | Total: 30 min

Ingredients:

1 lb shrimp, peeled and deveined
3 cups cooked brown rice
2 avocados, diced
1 cucumber, diced
1/2 red onion, finely chopped
1/4 cup soy sauce
2 tbsp sesame oil
1 tbsp honey
1 tsp ginger, grated
Juice of 1 lime
Sesame seeds for garnish
Salt and pepper to taste

Instructions:

In a bowl, whisk together soy sauce, sesame oil, honey, ginger, and lime juice.
In a skillet, cook shrimp over medium heat until pink and cooked through, seasoning with salt and pepper. Toss with half of the sauce.
Divide cooked brown rice among bowls. Top with cooked shrimp, diced avocado, cucumber, and red onion.
Drizzle with the remaining sauce.
Garnish with sesame seeds.
Serve immediately.

Nutritional Information (per serving):

Calories: Approximately 350 kcal
Protein: 25 g
Fat: 15 g
Carbohydrates: 35 g
Fiber: 6 g
Sugar: 6 g

186. Chicken Shawarma Pita

Prep: 20 min | Cook: 10 min | Total: 30 min

Ingredients:

1 lb chicken thighs, thinly sliced
6 pita bread
1 cup Greek yogurt
1 cucumber, diced
1 tomato, diced
1/2 red onion, thinly sliced
2 tbsp olive oil
2 tsp cumin
1 tsp paprika
1 tsp garlic powder
Salt and pepper to taste
Fresh parsley, chopped for garnish

Instructions:

In a bowl, mix together olive oil, cumin, paprika, garlic powder, salt, and pepper. Add chicken and marinate for at least 30 minutes.
Cook chicken in a skillet over medium heat until browned and cooked through.
Warm pita bread in the oven or on a skillet.
Spread Greek yogurt on each pita. Top with chicken, cucumber, tomato, and red onion.
Garnish with fresh parsley.
Serve immediately.

Nutritional Information (per serving, 1 pita):

Calories: Approximately 350 kcal
Protein: 25 g
Fat: 15 g
Carbohydrates: 35 g
Fiber: 4 g
Sugar: 5 g

187. Seared Salmon with Quinoa and Greens

Prep: 15 min | Cook: 15 min | Total: 30 min

Ingredients:

6 salmon fillets (4 oz each)
3 cups quinoa, cooked
6 cups mixed greens (spinach, kale, arugula)
2 tbsp olive oil
Salt and pepper to taste
Lemon wedges for serving

Instructions:

Season salmon fillets with salt and pepper.
Heat olive oil in a skillet over medium-high heat.
Sear salmon for 4-5 minutes on each side or until cooked to your liking.
Serve each salmon fillet over a bed of cooked quinoa and mixed greens.
Serve with a lemon wedge.
Store any leftovers in the refrigerator for up to 2 days.

Nutritional Information (per serving):

Calories: Approximately 350 kcal
Protein: 30 g
Fat: 15 g
Carbohydrates: 25 g
Fiber: 5 g
Sugar: 3 g

188. Pork Tenderloin with Roasted Vegetables

Prep: 20 min | Cook: 30 min | Total: 50 min

Ingredients:

2 lbs pork tenderloin
4 cups mixed vegetables (carrots, Brussels sprouts, sweet potatoes), chopped
2 tbsp olive oil
1 tsp rosemary
1 tsp thyme
Salt and pepper to taste

Instructions:

Preheat the oven to 375°F (190°C).
Season the pork tenderloin with rosemary, thyme, salt, and pepper.
In a separate bowl, toss the chopped vegetables with olive oil, salt, and pepper.
Place the pork tenderloin in the center of a baking sheet and surround it with the seasoned vegetables.
Roast for 25-30 minutes or until the pork reaches an internal temperature of 145°F (63°C).
Let the pork rest for a few minutes before slicing.
Serve with the roasted vegetables.
Store leftovers in the refrigerator for up to 3 days.

Nutritional Information (per serving):

Calories: Approximately 350 kcal
Protein: 30 g
Fat: 15 g
Carbohydrates: 20 g
Fiber: 5 g
Sugar: 5 g

189. Chicken Caprese Salad

Prep: 20 min | Cook: 10 min | Total: 30 min

Ingredients:

3 chicken breasts, grilled and sliced
6 cups mixed greens (such as spinach and arugula)
3 large tomatoes, sliced
1 ball fresh mozzarella cheese, sliced
1/4 cup balsamic vinegar
1/4 cup olive oil
Fresh basil leaves
Salt and pepper to taste

Instructions:

On a large platter, arrange mixed greens, sliced tomatoes, sliced mozzarella, and grilled chicken.
Drizzle with balsamic vinegar and olive oil.
Season with salt and pepper.
Garnish with fresh basil leaves.
Serve immediately or store in the refrigerator for up to 2 days.

Nutritional Information (per serving):

Calories: Approximately 350 kcal
Protein: 30 g
Fat: 20 g
Carbohydrates: 10 g
Fiber: 3 g
Sugar: 6 g

190. Beef and Vegetable Kebabs

Prep: 20 min | Cook: 10 min | Total: 30 min

Ingredients:

1.5 lbs beef sirloin, cut into cubes
2 bell peppers, cut into chunks
2 zucchini, sliced
1 onion, cut into chunks
2 tbsp olive oil
2 cloves garlic, minced
1 tsp paprika
Salt and pepper to taste
Wooden or metal skewers

Instructions:

In a bowl, mix olive oil, garlic, paprika, salt, and pepper. Marinate the beef cubes in this mixture for at least 30 minutes.
Preheat the grill to medium-high heat.
Thread beef, bell peppers, zucchini, and onions onto skewers.
Grill the kebabs, turning occasionally, until the beef is cooked to your liking and vegetables are tender, about 10-15 minutes.
Serve immediately.
Store any leftovers in the refrigerator for up to 3 days.

Nutritional Information (per serving, 2 kebabs):

Calories: Approximately 350 kcal
Protein: 30 g
Fat: 20 g
Carbohydrates: 10 g
Fiber: 2 g
Sugar: 6 g

191. Grilled Tuna Sandwich

Prep: 15 min | Cook: 5 min | Total: 20 min

Ingredients:

6 tuna steaks
12 slices whole grain bread
1/4 cup light mayonnaise
1 tbsp lemon juice
2 avocados, sliced
2 tomatoes, sliced
2 cups lettuce leaves
Salt and pepper to taste

Instructions:

Season tuna steaks with salt and pepper.
Grill the tuna steaks for 2-3 minutes per side or until cooked to your liking.
Mix mayonnaise with lemon juice. Spread on bread slices.
Assemble sandwiches with grilled tuna, avocado slices, tomato slices, and lettuce.
Serve immediately.
Store any leftover tuna in the refrigerator for up to 2 days.

Nutritional Information (per serving, 1 sandwich):

Calories: Approximately 350 kcal
Protein: 25 g
Fat: 15 g
Carbohydrates: 30 g
Fiber: 5 g
Sugar: 5 g

192. Chicken Alfredo Pasta

Prep: 10 min | Cook: 20 min | Total: 30 min

Ingredients:

12 oz whole wheat fettuccine
3 chicken breasts, grilled and sliced
2 cups broccoli florets
1 cup light Alfredo sauce
2 cloves garlic, minced
1 tbsp olive oil
Salt and pepper to taste
Grated Parmesan cheese for garnish

Instructions:

Cook fettuccine according to package instructions. Add broccoli in the last 3 minutes of cooking. Drain and set aside.
In a skillet, heat olive oil over medium heat. Sauté garlic until fragrant.
Add the cooked pasta, broccoli, and grilled chicken to the skillet. Pour Alfredo sauce over the mixture and toss to combine.
Season with salt and pepper.
Serve garnished with grated Parmesan cheese.
Store leftovers in the refrigerator for up to 3 days.

Nutritional Information (per serving):

Calories: Approximately 350 kcal
Protein: 30 g
Fat: 10 g
Carbohydrates: 40 g
Fiber: 5 g
Sugar: 3 g

193. Baked Lemon-Garlic Salmon

Prep: 10 min | Cook: 20 min | Total: 30 min

Ingredients:

6 salmon fillets (4 oz each)
2 lemons, 1 juiced and 1 sliced
4 cloves garlic, minced
2 tbsp olive oil
Salt and pepper to taste
Fresh dill for garnish

Instructions:

Preheat the oven to 400°F (200°C).
In a small bowl, mix together lemon juice, minced garlic, olive oil, salt, and pepper.
Place salmon fillets on a baking sheet lined with parchment paper.
Pour the lemon-garlic mixture over the salmon.
Top each fillet with a lemon slice.
Bake for 12-15 minutes, or until salmon is cooked through.
Garnish with fresh dill.
Store leftovers in the refrigerator for up to 2 days.

Nutritional Information (per serving, 1 fillet):

Calories: Approximately 300 kcal
Protein: 25 g
Fat: 20 g
Carbohydrates: 3 g
Fiber: 0.5 g
Sugar: 1 g

Vegan Dessert Recipes

194. VGN Avocado Chocolate Mousse

Prep: 10 min | Cook: 0 min | Total: 10 min + refrigeration

Ingredients:

4 ripe avocados, pitted and scooped
1/2 cup cocoa powder
1/2 cup maple syrup
1/4 cup almond milk
2 tsp vanilla extract
Pinch of salt

Instructions:

In a food processor, blend avocados until smooth.
Add cocoa powder, maple syrup, almond milk, vanilla extract, and a pinch of salt. Blend until creamy.
Refrigerate for at least 1 hour before serving.
Serve chilled, garnished with fruit or nuts if desired.
Store leftovers in the refrigerator for up to 2 days.

Nutritional Information (per serving):

Calories: Approximately 300 kcal
Protein: 4 g
Fat: 20 g
Carbohydrates: 30 g
Fiber: 10 g
Sugar: 15 g

195. VGN Baked Apples with Cinnamon

Prep: 10 min | Cook: 30 min | Total: 40 min

Ingredients:

6 large apples, cored
1/2 cup raisins
1/4 cup chopped walnuts
1/4 cup maple syrup
2 tsp cinnamon
1/4 cup water

Instructions:

Preheat the oven to 350°F (175°C).
Mix raisins, walnuts, maple syrup, and cinnamon in a bowl.
Fill each apple with the mixture and place in a baking dish.
Pour water into the bottom of the dish.
Bake for 30-35 minutes, until apples are tender.
Serve warm.
Store leftovers in the refrigerator for up to 3 days.

Nutritional Information (per serving, 1 apple):

Calories: Approximately 250 kcal
Protein: 2 g
Fat: 5 g
Carbohydrates: 50 g
Fiber: 6 g
Sugar: 40 g

196. VGN Berry Sorbet

Prep: 10 min | Cook: 0 min (Freeze overnight) | Total: 10 min + freezing

Ingredients:

4 cups mixed berries (fresh or frozen)
1/2 cup agave syrup or maple syrup
2 tbsp lemon juice
1/4 cup water

Instructions:

In a blender, combine mixed berries, agave syrup, lemon juice, and water. Blend until smooth.
Pour the mixture into a shallow pan and freeze until solid, about 4-6 hours.
Before serving, let the sorbet sit at room temperature for a few minutes to soften, then scoop and serve.
Store any leftovers in the freezer.

Nutritional Information (per serving):

Calories: Approximately 150 kcal
Protein: 1 g
Fat: 0 g
Carbohydrates: 35 g
Fiber: 5 g
Sugar: 30 g

197. VGN Coconut and Mango Rice Pudding

Prep: 5 min | Cook: 25 min | Total: 30 min

Ingredients:

1 cup Arborio rice
1 can (14 oz) coconut milk
2 cups almond milk
1/2 cup sugar
1 ripe mango, diced
1 tsp vanilla extract
Pinch of salt
Toasted coconut flakes for garnish

Instructions:

In a saucepan, combine rice, coconut milk, almond milk, and sugar. Stir well.
Cook over medium heat, stirring frequently, until the rice is tender and the mixture has thickened, about 25-30 minutes.
Remove from heat and stir in diced mango, vanilla extract, and a pinch of salt.
Serve warm or chilled, garnished with toasted coconut flakes.
Store leftovers in the refrigerator for up to 3 days.

Nutritional Information (per serving):

Calories: Approximately 300 kcal
Protein: 4 g
Fat: 10 g
Carbohydrates: 50 g
Fiber: 3 g
Sugar: 25 g

198. VGN Almond and Date Truffles

Prep: 20 min | Cook: 0 min | Total: 20 min + refrigeration

Ingredients:

1 cup dates, pitted
1/2 cup almonds
1/4 cup cocoa powder
1 tsp vanilla extract
Pinch of salt
Additional cocoa powder or shredded coconut for coating

Instructions:

In a food processor, blend dates and almonds until they form a sticky dough.
Add cocoa powder, vanilla extract, and a pinch of salt. Process until well combined.
Roll the mixture into small balls.
Coat each ball with additional cocoa powder or shredded coconut.
Refrigerate for at least 1 hour before serving.
Store in the refrigerator for up to 5 days.

Nutritional Information (per serving, 1 truffle):

Calories: Approximately 80 kcal
Protein: 2 g
Fat: 3 g
Carbohydrates: 12 g
Fiber: 2 g
Sugar: 9 g

199. VGN Roasted Peaches with Thyme

Prep: 10 min | Cook: 25 min | Total: 35 min

Ingredients:

6 peaches, halved and pitted
1/4 cup maple syrup
1 tsp fresh thyme, chopped
Pinch of salt
Vegan ice cream or whipped coconut cream for serving

Instructions:

Preheat the oven to 375°F (190°C).
Arrange peach halves cut-side up in a baking dish.
Drizzle with maple syrup and sprinkle with thyme and a pinch of salt.
Roast for 20-25 minutes, until peaches are tender and caramelized.
Serve warm with vegan ice cream or whipped coconut cream.
Store any leftovers in the refrigerator for up to 2 days.

Nutritional Information (per serving, 1 peach half):

Calories: Approximately 100 kcal
Protein: 1 g
Fat: 0.5 g
Carbohydrates: 25 g
Fiber: 2 g
Sugar: 22 g

200. VGN Banana and Oat Cookies

Prep: 15 min | Cook: 15 min | Total: 30 min

Ingredients:

3 ripe bananas, mashed
2 cups rolled oats
1/2 cup almond butter
1/4 cup maple syrup
1 tsp vanilla extract
1/2 tsp cinnamon
1/2 cup raisins or dark chocolate chips

Instructions:

Preheat the oven to 350°F (175°C).
In a large bowl, combine mashed bananas, rolled oats, almond butter, maple syrup, vanilla extract, and cinnamon.
Fold in raisins or chocolate chips.
Drop spoonfuls of the mixture onto a baking sheet lined with parchment paper.
Bake for 15-20 minutes, or until golden.
Let cool before serving.
Store in an airtight container at room temperature for up to 3 days.

Nutritional Information (per serving, 1 cookie):

Calories: Approximately 150 kcal
Protein: 4 g
Fat: 6 g
Carbohydrates: 20 g
Fiber: 3 g
Sugar: 10 g

201. VGN Chia Seed and Berry Pudding

Prep: 10 min | Cook: 0 min | Total: 10 min + refrigeration

Ingredients:

1/2 cup chia seeds
2 cups almond milk
1/4 cup maple syrup
1 tsp vanilla extract
2 cups mixed berries

Instructions:

In a bowl, mix chia seeds, almond milk, maple syrup, and vanilla extract.
Cover and refrigerate for at least 4 hours or overnight until the pudding thickens.
Serve topped with mixed berries.
Store leftovers in the refrigerator for up to 3 days.

Nutritional Information (per serving):

Calories: Approximately 200 kcal
Protein: 5 g
Fat: 8 g
Carbohydrates: 30 g
Fiber: 10 g
Sugar: 15 g

202. VGN Lemon Bars

Prep: 20 min | Cook: 25 min | Total: 45 min + refrigeration

Ingredients:

For the crust:
1 cup almond flour
1/4 cup coconut oil, melted
1/4 cup maple syrup
For the filling:
1/2 cup lemon juice
Zest of 2 lemons
1/2 cup maple syrup
1/4 cup cornstarch
1 1/2 cups water

Instructions:

Preheat the oven to 350°F (175°C).
Mix almond flour, coconut oil, and maple syrup for the crust. Press into the bottom of a lined baking dish.
Bake the crust for 10 minutes.
For the filling, whisk lemon juice, lemon zest, maple syrup, cornstarch, and water in a saucepan over medium heat. Stir until the mixture thickens.
Pour the filling over the baked crust and return to the oven for another 15 minutes.
Cool completely, then refrigerate for 2 hours before cutting into bars.
Store in the refrigerator for up to 3 days.

Nutritional Information (per serving, 1 bar):

Calories: Approximately 200 kcal
Protein: 3 g
Fat: 10 g
Carbohydrates: 25 g
Fiber: 3 g
Sugar: 15 g

203. VGN Baked Pears with Walnuts

Prep: 10 min | Cook: 25 min | Total: 35 min

Ingredients:

6 ripe pears, halved and cored
1/2 cup walnuts, chopped
1/4 cup maple syrup
1 tsp cinnamon
1/2 tsp nutmeg
1/4 cup plant-based yogurt for serving

Instructions:

Preheat the oven to 350°F (175°C).
Arrange pear halves cut-side up on a baking sheet.
Mix walnuts, maple syrup, cinnamon, and nutmeg in a bowl. Spoon this mixture into the center of each pear half.
Bake for 20-25 minutes, or until pears are soft.
Serve warm with a dollop of plant-based yogurt.
Store any leftovers in the refrigerator for up to 2 days.

Nutritional Information (per serving, 1 pear half):

Calories: Approximately 150 kcal
Protein: 2 g
Fat: 5 g
Carbohydrates: 25 g
Fiber: 4 g
Sugar: 18 g

204. VGN Dark Chocolate-Dipped Strawberries

Prep: 15 min | Cook: 5 min | Total: 20 min + refrigeration

Ingredients:

24 strawberries, washed and dried
8 oz dark chocolate, vegan
1 tbsp coconut oil

Instructions:

Melt dark chocolate and coconut oil together in a double boiler or microwave, stirring until smooth.
Dip each strawberry into the chocolate, coating it about halfway.
Place dipped strawberries on a baking sheet lined with parchment paper.
Refrigerate until the chocolate sets, about 30 minutes.
Store in the refrigerator for up to 2 days.

Nutritional Information (per serving, 1 strawberry):

Calories: Approximately 70 kcal
Protein: 1 g
Fat: 4 g
Carbohydrates: 8 g
Fiber: 1 g
Sugar: 6 g

205. VGN Carrot Cupcakes

Prep: 20 min | Cook: 25 min | Total: 45 min

Ingredients:

2 cups all-purpose flour
1 cup sugar
1 tsp baking powder
1/2 tsp baking soda
1 tsp cinnamon
1/2 tsp nutmeg
1/4 cup vegetable oil
1/4 cup applesauce
1/4 cup almond milk
2 cups grated carrots
1/2 cup raisins
1/2 cup walnuts, chopped

Instructions:

Preheat the oven to 350°F (175°C). Line a cupcake tin with paper liners.
In a bowl, mix flour, sugar, baking powder, baking soda, cinnamon, and nutmeg.
Stir in vegetable oil, applesauce, and almond milk until combined.
Fold in grated carrots, raisins, and walnuts.
Fill each cupcake liner about 2/3 full with batter.
Bake for 20-25 minutes, or until a toothpick inserted into the center comes out clean.
Cool before serving.
Store in an airtight container for up to 3 days.

Nutritional Information (per serving, 1 cupcake):

Calories: Approximately 200 kcal
Protein: 3 g
Fat: 8 g
Carbohydrates: 30 g
Fiber: 2 g
Sugar: 18 g

206. VGN Grilled Pineapple with Mint

Prep: 5 min | Cook: 10 min | Total: 15 min

Ingredients:

1 large pineapple, peeled and cut into slices
2 tbsp maple syrup
1 tbsp lime juice
1/4 cup fresh mint, chopped

Instructions:

Preheat a grill or grill pan to medium heat.
Brush pineapple slices with a mixture of maple syrup and lime juice.
Grill the pineapple slices for 2-3 minutes per side, or until they have nice grill marks.
Transfer to a serving platter and sprinkle with chopped mint.
Serve warm or at room temperature.
Store any leftovers in the refrigerator for up to 2 days.

Nutritional Information (per serving, 1 pineapple slice):

Calories: Approximately 70 kcal
Protein: 0.5 g
Fat: 0 g
Carbohydrates: 18 g
Fiber: 2 g
Sugar: 16 g

207. VGN Chocolate Avocado Brownies

Prep: 15 min | Cook: 25 min | Total: 40 min

Ingredients:

2 ripe avocados, mashed
1 cup all-purpose flour
1/2 cup cocoa powder
1 cup sugar
1/2 cup plant-based milk
1 tsp vanilla extract
1/2 tsp baking powder
1/4 tsp salt
1/2 cup dark chocolate chips, vegan

Instructions:

Preheat the oven to 350°F (175°C). Line an 8-inch square baking pan with parchment paper.
In a large bowl, combine mashed avocados, flour, cocoa powder, sugar, plant-based milk, vanilla extract, baking powder, and salt. Mix until smooth.
Fold in dark chocolate chips.
Spread the batter evenly in the prepared pan.
Bake for 25-30 minutes, or until a toothpick inserted into the center comes out clean.
Cool before cutting into squares.
Store in an airtight container for up to 3 days.

Nutritional Information (per serving, 1 brownie square):

Calories: Approximately 200 kcal
Protein: 3 g
Fat: 10 g
Carbohydrates: 28 g
Fiber: 4 g
Sugar: 16 g

208. VGN Mixed Berry Compote

Prep: 5 min | Cook: 10 min | Total: 15 min

Ingredients:

4 cups mixed berries (strawberries, blueberries, raspberries)
1/4 cup sugar
1 tbsp lemon juice
1 tsp vanilla extract

Instructions:

In a saucepan, combine mixed berries, sugar, and lemon juice.
Cook over medium heat, stirring occasionally, until the berries release their juices and the mixture thickens, about 10-15 minutes. Remove from heat and stir in vanilla extract. Serve warm or cool. Can be used as a topping for vegan ice cream or pancakes.
Store leftovers in the refrigerator for up to 3 days.

Nutritional Information (per serving, 1/2 cup):

Calories: Approximately 100 kcal
Protein: 1 g
Fat: 0.5 g
Carbohydrates: 25 g
Fiber: 4 g
Sugar: 20 g

Vegetarian Dessert Recipes

Prep: 10 min | Cook: 5 min (Set for 4 hours) | Total: 15 min + refrigeration

Ingredients:

2 cups Greek yogurt
1 cup almond milk
1/4 cup honey, plus more for drizzling
1 tsp vanilla extract
2 tsp gelatin powder
1/4 cup water

Instructions:

Sprinkle gelatin over water in a small bowl. Let it sit for 5 minutes to bloom.
Heat almond milk in a saucepan over medium heat. Do not boil. Add bloomed gelatin and stir until dissolved.
Remove from heat and stir in Greek yogurt, honey, and vanilla extract.
Pour the mixture into 6 dessert cups. Refrigerate for at least 4 hours or until set.
Serve with a drizzle of honey on top.
Store any leftovers in the refrigerator for up to 2 days.

Nutritional Information (per serving):

Calories: Approximately 150 kcal
Protein: 10 g
Fat: 3 g
Carbohydrates: 20 g
Fiber: 0 g
Sugar: 18 g

Prep: 10 min | Cook: 0 min | Total: 10 min

Ingredients:

2 cups ricotta cheese
2 cups mixed berries (strawberries, blueberries, raspberries)
1/4 cup honey
1 tsp lemon zest
1/2 tsp vanilla extract
Mint leaves for garnish

Instructions:

In a bowl, mix ricotta cheese with honey, lemon zest, and vanilla extract until smooth.
Layer the ricotta mixture and mixed berries in 6 serving glasses.
Garnish with mint leaves.
Serve immediately or refrigerate until ready to serve.
Store any leftovers in the refrigerator for up to 2 days.

Nutritional Information (per serving):

Calories: Approximately 200 kcal
Protein: 10 g
Fat: 8 g
Carbohydrates: 25 g
Fiber: 2 g
Sugar: 20 g

211. VGT Baked Ricotta with Lemon and Thyme

Prep: 10 min | Cook: 25 min | Total: 35 min

Ingredients:

2 cups ricotta cheese
1 lemon, zested and juiced
2 tbsp honey
1 tbsp fresh thyme leaves
Salt and pepper to taste

Instructions:

Preheat the oven to 350°F (175°C).
In a bowl, combine ricotta, lemon zest, lemon juice, honey, thyme, salt, and pepper.
Transfer to a baking dish and smooth the top.
Bake for 25-30 minutes, until slightly golden.
Serve warm.
Store leftovers in the refrigerator for up to 2 days.

Nutritional Information (per serving):

Calories: Approximately 180 kcal
Protein: 12 g
Fat: 10 g
Carbohydrates: 12 g
Fiber: 0 g
Sugar: 10 g

212. VGT Honey and Almond Poached Pears

Prep: 10 min | Cook: 25 min | Total: 35 min

Ingredients:

6 pears, peeled, halved, and cored
4 cups water
1/2 cup honey
1 vanilla bean, split and seeds scraped
1 cinnamon stick
1/2 cup almonds, slivered

Instructions:

In a large saucepan, combine water, honey, vanilla bean (including seeds), and cinnamon stick. Bring to a simmer.
Add pear halves to the saucepan. Simmer gently for 15-20 minutes or until pears are tender.
Remove pears from the liquid and let cool.
Reduce the remaining liquid by half until it thickens into a syrup.
Serve pears with syrup and sprinkle with slivered almonds.
Store any leftovers in the refrigerator for up to 3 days.

Nutritional Information (per serving, 1 pear half):

Calories: Approximately 200 kcal
Protein: 2 g
Fat: 4 g
Carbohydrates: 40 g
Fiber: 6 g
Sugar: 30 g

213. VGT Light Cheesecake with Berry Compote

Prep: 20 min | Cook: 45 min | Total: 1 hr 5 min + refrigeration

Ingredients:

For the crust:
1 cup graham cracker crumbs
2 tbsp butter, melted
For the filling:
2 cups low-fat cream cheese
1/2 cup sugar
2 eggs
1 tsp vanilla extract
For the compote:
2 cups mixed berries
1/4 cup sugar
1 tbsp lemon juice

Instructions:

Preheat the oven to 325°F (165°C). Mix graham cracker crumbs and melted butter, press into the bottom of a springform pan.
In a bowl, beat cream cheese, sugar, eggs, and vanilla until smooth. Pour over crust.
Bake for 45 minutes or until set. Cool and then refrigerate for at least 4 hours.
For the compote, combine berries, sugar, and lemon juice in a saucepan. Cook over medium heat until berries break down and the mixture thickens.
Serve cheesecake with berry compote on top.
Store in the refrigerator for up to 3 days.

Nutritional Information (per serving, 1 slice):

Calories: Approximately 300 kcal
Protein: 6 g
Fat: 18 g
Carbohydrates: 30 g
Fiber: 2 g
Sugar: 22 g

214. VGT Zucchini and Chocolate Chip Muffins

Prep: 15 min | Cook: 20 min | Total: 35 min

Ingredients:

2 cups whole wheat flour
1/2 cup sugar
1 tsp baking soda
1 tsp cinnamon
1/2 tsp salt
1 cup zucchini, grated
1/2 cup unsweetened applesauce
1/4 cup vegetable oil
2 eggs
1 tsp vanilla extract
1/2 cup dark chocolate chips

Instructions:

Preheat the oven to 350°F (175°C). Line a muffin tin with paper liners.
In a large bowl, combine flour, sugar, baking soda, cinnamon, and salt.
Stir in zucchini, applesauce, oil, eggs, and vanilla.
Fold in chocolate chips.
Fill muffin cups about 2/3 full with the batter.
Bake for 20-25 minutes, or until a toothpick inserted into the center comes out clean.
Cool before serving.
Store in an airtight container for up to 3 days.

Nutritional Information (per serving, 1 muffin):

Calories: Approximately 200 kcal
Protein: 4 g
Fat: 8 g
Carbohydrates: 30 g
Fiber: 3 g
Sugar: 15 g

215. VGT Yogurt and Mixed Berry Trifle

Prep: 20 min | Cook: 0 min | Total: 20 min

Ingredients:

3 cups Greek yogurt
1/4 cup honey
1 tsp vanilla extract
2 cups mixed berries (strawberries, blueberries, raspberries)
4 cups angel food cake, cubed
Fresh mint leaves for garnish

Instructions:

In a bowl, mix Greek yogurt with honey and vanilla extract.
In serving glasses, layer angel food cake cubes, Greek yogurt mixture, and mixed berries.
Repeat the layers until glasses are filled.
Garnish with fresh mint leaves.
Serve immediately or refrigerate until ready to serve.
Store any leftovers in the refrigerator for up to 2 days.

Nutritional Information (per serving):

Calories: Approximately 300 kcal
Protein: 10 g
Fat: 3 g
Carbohydrates: 55 g
Fiber: 4 g
Sugar: 40 g

216. VGT Baked Custard with Nutmeg

Prep: 10 min | Cook: 40 min | Total: 50 min

Ingredients:

6 eggs
1/4 cup sugar
1 tsp vanilla extract
4 cups low-fat milk
1/2 tsp ground nutmeg
Fresh berries for garnish

Instructions:

Preheat the oven to 350°F (175°C).
In a large bowl, whisk together eggs, sugar, and vanilla extract.
Heat milk in a saucepan until just warm. Gradually add to the egg mixture, stirring continuously.
Pour the mixture into 6 ramekins. Sprinkle with nutmeg.
Place ramekins in a baking dish and fill the dish with hot water halfway up the sides of the ramekins.
Bake for 30-35 minutes or until custards are set.
Cool before serving. Garnish with fresh berries.
Store leftovers in the refrigerator for up to 3 days.

Nutritional Information (per serving, 1 ramekin):

Calories: Approximately 200 kcal
Protein: 10 g
Fat: 8 g
Carbohydrates: 20 g
Fiber: 0 g
Sugar: 20 g

217. VGT Fruit Salad with Lime and Mint Dressing

Prep: 15 min | Cook: 0 min | Total: 15 min

Ingredients:

2 cups strawberries, hulled and sliced
2 cups blueberries
2 cups pineapple, diced
2 kiwis, peeled and sliced
1/4 cup fresh lime juice
2 tbsp honey
1/4 cup fresh mint leaves, chopped

Instructions:

In a large bowl, combine strawberries, blueberries, pineapple, and kiwis.
In a small bowl, whisk together lime juice and honey.
Pour the dressing over the fruit and toss gently.
Sprinkle with chopped mint leaves.
Serve chilled.
Store leftovers in the refrigerator for up to 2 days.

Nutritional Information (per serving, 1 cup):

Calories: Approximately 100 kcal
Protein: 1 g
Fat: 0.5 g
Carbohydrates: 25 g
Fiber: 4 g
Sugar: 18 g

218. VGT Lemon and Lavender Yogurt Cake

Prep: 15 min | Cook: 45 min | Total: 1 hr

Ingredients:

2 cups all-purpose flour
1/2 cup sugar
1 tsp baking powder
1/2 tsp baking soda
1/4 tsp salt
1 cup Greek yogurt
1/2 cup olive oil
2 tbsp lemon juice
Zest of 1 lemon
2 tsp dried lavender flowers

Instructions:

Preheat the oven to 350°F (175°C). Grease a loaf pan.
In a bowl, whisk together flour, sugar, baking powder, baking soda, and salt.
In another bowl, mix Greek yogurt, olive oil, lemon juice, and lemon zest.
Combine wet and dry ingredients. Fold in lavender flowers.
Pour the batter into the prepared pan and bake for 45-50 minutes, or until a toothpick inserted into the center comes out clean.
Cool before slicing.
Store in an airtight container for up to 3 days.

Nutritional Information (per serving, 1 slice):

Calories: Approximately 250 kcal
Protein: 5 g
Fat: 12 g
Carbohydrates: 30 g
Fiber: 1 g
Sugar: 15 g

219. VGT Strawberry and Basil Granita

Prep: 15 min | Cook: 0 min (Freeze) | Total: 15 min + freezing

Ingredients:

4 cups strawberries, hulled
1/2 cup sugar
1/4 cup water
2 tbsp fresh basil, chopped
Juice of 1 lemon

Instructions:

In a saucepan, dissolve sugar in water over medium heat. Let cool.
In a blender, puree strawberries with the sugar syrup, lemon juice, and basil.
Pour the mixture into a shallow dish and freeze.
Every 30 minutes, scrape with a fork to create a flaky texture. Repeat until completely frozen.
Serve chilled.
Store in the freezer.

Nutritional Information (per serving, 1 cup):

Calories: Approximately 100 kcal
Protein: 1 g
Fat: 0 g
Carbohydrates: 25 g
Fiber: 3 g
Sugar: 20 g

220. VGT Roasted Figs with Honey

Prep: 10 min | Cook: 15 min | Total: 25 min

Ingredients:

12 fresh figs, halved
1/4 cup honey
2 tbsp balsamic vinegar
1/4 tsp ground cinnamon
Fresh thyme for garnish

Instructions:

Preheat the oven to 350°F (175°C).
Arrange fig halves cut-side up on a baking sheet.
Drizzle with honey and balsamic vinegar.
Sprinkle with cinnamon.
Roast for 20-25 minutes, or until figs are soft and caramelized.
Garnish with fresh thyme leaves before serving.
Store any leftovers in the refrigerator for up to 2 days.

Nutritional Information (per serving, 2 fig halves):

Calories: Approximately 100 kcal
Protein: 1 g
Fat: 0.5 g
Carbohydrates: 25 g
Fiber: 3 g
Sugar: 20 g

221. VGT Low-Calorie Tiramisu

Prep: 30 min | Cook: 0 min (Chill) | Total: 30 min + refrigeration

Ingredients:

2 cups strong coffee, cooled
1/2 cup mascarpone cheese
1/2 cup Greek yogurt
1/4 cup xylitol
1 tsp vanilla extract
24 ladyfingers
Cocoa powder for dusting

Instructions:

In a bowl, whisk together mascarpone, Greek yogurt, sugar, and vanilla extract.
Briefly dip ladyfingers in coffee and layer in a dish.
Spread half of the mascarpone mixture over the ladyfingers.
Add another layer of coffee-dipped ladyfingers and top with the remaining mascarpone mixture.
Refrigerate for at least 4 hours or overnight.
Dust with cocoa powder before serving.
Store in the refrigerator for up to 3 days.

Nutritional Information (per serving, 1 piece):

Calories: Approximately 150 kcal
Protein: 4 g
Fat: 6 g
Carbohydrates: 20 g
Fiber: 0 g
Sugar: 3 g

222. VGT Baked Nectarines with Vanilla

Prep: 10 min | Cook: 25 min | Total: 35 min

Ingredients:

6 nectarines, halved and pitted
1/4 cup honey
1 vanilla bean, split and seeds scraped
1/4 cup almond slices
A pinch of cinnamon

Instructions:

Preheat the oven to 375°F (190°C).
Place nectarine halves cut-side up in a baking dish.
Drizzle with honey and sprinkle with vanilla seeds and cinnamon.
Bake for 20-25 minutes, or until nectarines are tender and juicy.
Garnish with almond slices before serving.
Store any leftovers in the refrigerator for up to 2 days.

Nutritional Information (per serving, 1 nectarine half):

Calories: Approximately 100 kcal
Protein: 1 g
Fat: 2 g
Carbohydrates: 20 g
Fiber: 2 g
Sugar: 18 g

223. VGT Apple and Cinnamon Yogurt Cake

Prep: 20 min | Cook: 40 min | Total: 1 hr

Ingredients:

2 cups whole wheat flour
1/2 cup sugar
1 tsp baking powder
1/2 tsp baking soda
1 tsp cinnamon
1/4 cup vegetable oil
1 cup Greek yogurt
2 eggs
1 tsp vanilla extract
2 apples, peeled and diced

Instructions:

Preheat the oven to 350°F (175°C). Grease a cake pan.
In a large bowl, mix flour, sugar, baking powder, baking soda, and cinnamon.
In another bowl, whisk together oil, yogurt, eggs, and vanilla.
Combine the wet and dry ingredients. Fold in diced apples.
Pour the batter into the prepared pan and bake for 35-40 minutes, or until a toothpick inserted into the center comes out clean.
Cool before serving.
Store in an airtight container for up to 3 days.

Nutritional Information (per serving, 1 slice):

Calories: Approximately 200 kcal
Protein: 4 g
Fat: 8 g
Carbohydrates: 30 g
Fiber: 3 g
Sugar: 15 g

Made in the USA
Las Vegas, NV
29 December 2024